THE KAPPA ALPHA ORDER

1865-1897

"Should Esau sell his birthright for a mess of potage?"

The Kappa Alpha Order

1865-1897

How It Came to Be Southern

Gary Thomas Scott

HERITAGE BOOKS
2007

HERITAGE BOOKS
AN IMPRINT OF HERITAGE BOOKS, INC.

Books, CDs, and more—Worldwide

For our listing of thousands of titles see our website at
www.HeritageBooks.com

Published 2007 by
HERITAGE BOOKS, INC.
Publishing Division
65 East Main Street
Westminster, Maryland 21157-5026

Copyright © 1994 Gary Thomas Scott

Other books by the author:
CD: The Kappa Alpha Order, 1865-1897: How It Came to Be Southern

All rights reserved. No part of this book may be reproduced or transmitted in any form or by any means, electronic or mechanical, including photocopying, recording or by any information storage and retrieval system without written permission from the author, except for the inclusion of brief quotations in a review.

International Standard Book Number: 978-0-7884-0008-7

TO

WILLIAM E. FORESTER

EXECUTIVE VICE PRESIDENT

KAPPA ALPHA ORDER

Contents

Illustrations	ix
Introduction	xi
Preface	1

Chapter

I. The Founding	3
II. Institutional and Structural Development, 1870-1897	25
III. The Romantic Mind of the K.A.O.	43
IV. The Phantom of Northern Extension	61
V. The Lost Cause, Southern History, and Robert E. Lee	75
VI. The Mind of the New South	89

Appendix

A. Chapter List, 1865-1899	95
B. Founding Date of Kappa Alpha	99
Notes	105
Bibliography	121

New Coat of Arms.

*From
Kappa Alpha Journal
May 1897*

Illustrations

	Page
Main Building, Washington and Lee Campus	4
Founders of Kappa Alpha Order	8
Dr. Samuel Zenas Ammen	11
Ann Smith Academy	16
Alpha Chapter, 1867	19
Gamma Chapter, 1893	24
Chi Chapter, 1893	29
Kappa Alpha Journal Advertisement, 1889	34
Alpha Alpha Chapter's House, 1891	38
Xi Chapter's House, 1896	40
Army of Templars Crossing a River	42
Knights Raising Red Cross Standard	50
Pope Urban II Preaching the First Crusade	53
Admission of a Novice to the Vows of the Order of the Temple	54
Alpha Delta Chapter, 1894	69
General Robert E. Lee	84
The Conquered Banner	87
Engraving, untitled	93

Introduction

This work came out of a master's thesis that I prepared at the University of North Carolina at Chapel Hill during the campus upheavals of the late 1960s. It was conceived in graduate seminars of Dr. George Brown Tindall and Dr. Joel Williamson in partial completion of my master's degree in Southern history in 1969. At the same time I was writing the thesis I was deeply involved in campus protests and the civil rights demonstrations that were precipitated by the death of Dr. Martin Luther King, Jr. The words as I read them nearly 25 years later have the ring of the militancy of that period.

In 1963 Kappa Alpha Order authorized individual chapters on university campuses to waive racial restrictions as a condition for membership if so required by university. Then, in 1971 Kappa Alpha completely removed its racial restrictive membership clause. In 1974 I was present at Johns Hopkins University, Alpha Lambda Chapter, Baltimore, Maryland for the initiation of Peter Townsend, one of the first African American members of the Kappa Alpha Order.

In 1986 the Order moved its headquarters to Lexington, Virginia, its place of founding. After an absence of more than a century Kappa Alpha offices are now near Washington and Lee University, the Virginia Military Institute, and the graves of Samuel Zenas Ammen and Robert E. Lee.

While retaining its fondness for Lee and its early Southern origins, Kappa Alpha Order now includes in its membership men from every racial, ethnic, and religious background. Northern chapters exist at Purdue and Princeton Universities, Miami of Ohio, and Penn State.

In preparing this manuscript I had the constant support and assistance of William E. Forester, formerly Executive Secretary and now Executive Vice President, Kappa Alpha Order, and Knight Commanders Henry J. Foresman and Richard T. Feller.

Gary Thomas Scott
Washington, D.C.
1993

Preface

In his intriguing essay entitled "Southern Mythology," Professor George Brown Tindall of the University of North Carolina suggests that perhaps a useful method in trying to understand the South would be to study the mythology which has grown up about the region. In using the idea of "social myth," Tindall makes it clear that he is not referring to an illusion or a piece of exploded fantasy. Rather, to him social myths are "mental pictures that portray the pattern of what a people think they are (or ought to be) or what somebody else thinks they are."[1] He sees them as an attempt at reducing the aspirations and abstractions of a people into concrete and dramatic imagery, and he understands "social myths" as having various functions:

> "A myth," Mark Schorer has observed, "is a large, controlling image that gives philosophical meaning to the facts of ordinary life, that is, which has organizing value for experience." It may offer useful generalizations by which data may be tested. But being also "charged with values, aspirations, ideals, and meanings," myths may become the ground for belief, for either loyalty and defense on the one hand or hostility and opposition of the other. In such circumstances, a myth itself becomes one of the realities of history, significantly influencing the course of human action, for good or ill. There is, of course, always a danger of illusion, a danger that in ordering one's vision of reality, the myth may predetermine the categories of perception, rendering one blind to things that do not fit into the mental image.[2]

Thus, having given the reader a definition of social myth, Tindall proceeds to discuss some of the myths of "Southernism," the Plantation myth, the Agrarian myth, the Confederate myth, the myth of the Savage South, and the myth of the New South being among them, and he concludes by suggesting that historians may well find a fruitful harvest in turning to the study of Southern mythology in the unending quest for the "central theme of Southern history."

The present study is an attempt to view a remnant of "Southern mythology" in the early history of a distinctively Southern postbellum organization, a college fraternity, known as the Kappa Alpha Order.

Most of the standard histories of Greek letter societies in America, be they one volume studies such as Farr's *Kappa Sigma, A History*, or William C. Levere's multi-volume *History of Sigma Alpha Epsilon*, have generally been devoted to the story of the structural growth and chapter expansion of their respective organizations.

1

These histories, so often written by elderly alumni, tend to soar off into filiopietistic flights of praise about the founders of said organizations and about the noble principles which said founders sought to promulgate. Such is not my purpose here. Nor is it my purpose to present in encyclopedic fashion, an institutional history of Kappa Alpha. The story of chapter expansion in the South has been largely ignored, and except for a detailed recounting of the founding and earliest history of the fraternity, the structural development of the organization has been treated in summary fashion.

This work is primarily an attempt at answering several simple questions: How and why did Kappa Alpha Order, one of several college fraternities established in the South after the Civil War, come to see itself as an organization devoted to the preservation of certain Southern "ideals and principles," i.e. myths or folk attitudes? What were these myths or attitudes which the fraternity sought to preserve? How did KA aid in the portage of these attitudes from one generation to another? And how, in turn, did these selected attitudes work to shape the organization? I hope that this attempt to decipher "the mind of the Kappa Alpha Fraternity" will shed some light on the "mind of the New South."

Chapter I

✛   ✛   ✛

THE FOUNDING

Main Building - Washington and Lee University
Lexington, Virginia

From
History and Catalogue of the Kappa Alpha Fraternity
Nashville, Tennessee
1891

Between the Alleghenies to the west and the Blue Ridge Mountains to the east lies a valley that stretches the entire length of western Virginia. With an average width of ten to fifteen miles, the valley is composed of rolling farm lands of dark red clay, interspersed with stretches of pine and hardwood forest, all of which is drained by a profusion of rivers and streams. From any prospect upon the valley floor it is possible to perceive the outline of the mountains on either side, which to the viewer seem to rise in the distance from every direction. To the north from Winchester to Staunton, because of the river which meanders along its floor, the valley is called the Valley of the Shenandoah. To the south around Lexington, the valley is known by a more general designation as the Valley of Virginia.

In early October 1865, James Ward Wood, a twenty year old former Confederate soldier of romantic inclinations, traveled down the Valley of Virginia from his home in Hardy County, West Virginia. His destination was Washington College, an impoverished, ramshackle school of former Presbyterian affiliation located in Lexington, Virginia. Once there, Wood enrolled as a Freshman.[1]

Although it had existed under various names in the Valley of Virginia since 1749, Washington College had barely managed to survive the Civil War. In 1864, a Federal raiding party under the command of General David Hunter entered Lexington, looted the college and left its buildings in a bad state of repair, and burned the Virginia Military Institute, a few blocks away. Most of the student body had vanished during the war, and at the cessation of hostilities in 1865, only four faculty members remained.

By the fall of 1865, the citizens of Lexington had reason to hope for the future success of their small college. In early August that year, the Board of Trustees of Washington College had taken a bold step. It invited General Robert Edward Lee to become the president of their poverty stricken institution. To the astonishment of the entire South, Lee accepted.

As president of Washington College, Lee was to bring the liberalizing effect of his Virginia Tidewater background to counterbalance the stern Calvinistic influence of the Scotch-Irish Presbyterians that had dominated the college for years. That strict Calvinism had been a prevailing force in the Valley of Virginia. It was embodied by the life of General Thomas Jonathan "Stonewall" Jackson, who had been a professor of mathematics at the Virginia Military Institute before the Civil War. In 1865, Jackson's body lay buried in the Lexington cemetery. Lee, on the other hand, arrived in Lexington with the understanding that the sectarian affiliation of Washington

College would cease, a point to which the college trustees had readily agreed in their desire to secure Lee's acceptance of the presidency of the college.

After he assumed the duties of his new office, Lee quickly abolished all rules regulating student conduct, including the restrictions against secret fraternities, and established in their place only one regulation — each member of the all-male student population must at all times be a gentleman.[2] The Board of Trustees of Washington College eagerly complied with General Lee's wishes, because they knew that the reputation of his name would attract a much-needed student body and much-needed funds for the college endowment.

So, James Ward Wood of Hardy County, West Virginia, traveled down the Valley of Virginia to Washington College in Lexington. He, as did many other former Confederate soldiers, went there "to be taught by the man under whom they had fought."[3]

Four generations of the Wood family had lived in Hardy County, West Virginia as middle class farmers and slave holders.[4] When the Civil War broke out, the Woods sided with the South, and young James Ward Wood joined a Confederate cavalry regiment. Wood's military career ended several months before the fall of the Confederacy. Late in the war, while at home on furlough, Wood rode out to call upon a young lady with a pistol carelessly stuck in his bootleg. As he was mounting his horse, the pistol accidentally fired, and Wood received a severe leg wound. Consequently, the young Confederate soldier spent the last few months of the war at home, nursing his wound.[5] Although the wound eventually healed, Wood walked with a slight limp for the rest of his life.[6]

During the final months of the war and through the summer of 1865, Wood remained at home to convalesce. He spent many nights loafing at a country store, listening to the stories of a character named Van Arsdale. Van Arsdale, who was a member of the Masonic Lodge, the Royal Arch Masons, and other sundry secret organizations, held his audience's attention by vividly describing the ritualism, oaths, and awful mysteries of secret societies.[7] These lurid descriptions, recounted in the black of night, kindled in Wood's mind a fascination for the esoteric. As a result, during the months before he left for Lexington, the young, lame, former Confederate soldier spent much of his time reading his father's books on Masonry and dreaming of mystic symbols, secret initiations, and fraternal splendor.[8]

When he arrived in Lexington in early October, James Ward Wood found a room at the large country home of the Tutwiler family about a mile south of town.[9] In the meantime, the Reverend John A. Scott, a Presbyterian minister, had recently moved with his family to Lexington in order to educate his two sons, William Nelson and Stanhope McClelland Scott, at Washington College. To provide for his family while his sons were in school, Reverend Scott had accepted the position of principal of the Ann Smith Academy, a girls' finishing school in Lexington. The Wood and Scott families had been close friends in Hardy County for generations; and as Mrs. Tutwiler was Mrs. Scott's sister, the Scott family often visited at the Tutwiler house. Thus, James Ward Wood found himself in the company of the two Scott brothers almost immediately after he arrived in Lexington.[10]

During his first few days at school, Wood saw a large gold medal annually awarded for scholastic excellence on display in the registrar's office. He exclaimed with determination, "I'm going to have one."[11] Still, he spent little time at his studies during his first year at Washington College. Although rustic and unsophisticated, Wood had done much reading in his earlier years. He had a fair command of the English language and he often quoted from the Bible, which remained his favorite book. Wood, however, lacked the mind for disciplined study, and he consequently spent much of his time writing poetry and indulging in lofty speculation.

> He was in fact a walking dreamer, seeing behind a fact another fact behind the thing, a symbol; ghost behind ghost, in endless series. In a sense he "lived seeing the invisible", finding the actual world prosy in comparison with the romantic world which lies behind it.[12]

Mystic symbols fascinated Wood, and often, he repeated over and over foreign words which he did not understand, as if working a magical incantation.[13] Hearing that secret fraternities existed at Washington College, Wood resolved to join one.

During the Civil War, the college fraternity system had completely died out in the South. Several fraternities had existed at Washington College before the war, in spite of college regulations against them. As the new college president, Lee removed the regulations against secret organizations.[14] Immediately thereafter, in the fall of 1865, Phi Kappa Psi and Beta Theta Pi quickly re-established their chapters on the Washington College campus. They were joined in November 1865 by Alpha Tau Omega, a new fraternity that had been founded at the nearby Virginia Military Institute.[15] Although it may never be known for certain, in all probability James Ward Wood attempted to join one, or all, of the three existing fraternities shortly after he arrived in Lexington, only to receive a cold rebuff from each of them.[16]

Judge James Ward Wood

From
The Kappa Alpha Journal
May 1898

Rev. William Nelson Scott, D. D.

From
The Kappa Alpha Journal
May 1898

Stanhope McClelland Scott, M. D.

From
The Kappa Alpha Journal
May 1898

To add to his perplexities, during the Christmas season of 1865, Wood had gone up to Brownsburg, a few miles north of Lexington, to see a certain Miss Johnstone. He took with him a very large emerald ring, hoping to win the lady's hand. Miss Johnstone proved fickle, and Wood returned to Lexington disheartened.[17] Thus rejected both in love and by the existing fraternal societies at Washington College, young Wood decided to create his own fraternity.

Because he lived over a mile out in the country from the college, Wood spent much of his time between classes loafing in the room of William Archibald Walsh. Walsh, who was from Richmond, Virginia, lived in the southernmost room of the old South Dormitory. The dormitory consisted of a long row of one-story rooms and extended from the south side of the college building toward a professor's residence, a structure which has long since been replaced by Newcomb Hall.[18] William Nelson Scott frequently met Wood in Walsh's room, and the three became friends.

On 21 December 1865, at a supper in Walsh's room, that was attended by Walsh, James Ward Wood, and William Nelson Scott, Wood rose and proposed a toast to "the two Williams."[19] Either at that time or at some later date, while sitting in Walsh's room, Wood suggested to William Nelson Scott that they organize a new fraternity.[20] Wood included Walsh in the idea as well as Scott's younger brother, Stanhope McClelland Scott, who entered Washington College in January 1866.[21] Sometime between late December 1865, and early spring of 1866, the four of them swore together in the founding of the Phi Kappa Chi Fraternity. Wood devised the name, probably as a parody of Phi Kappa Psi, one of the fraternities at Washington College that had refused membership to Wood. (See Appendix B.)

Wood's new fraternity did not spring forth overnight. Wood knew from his previous study of secret organizations that an initiation ceremony had to be devised complete with secret symbols, oaths, mottoes, and passwords, as well as a constitution and a badge. From an unknown source Wood obtained the manuscript ritual of a defunct antebellum fraternity,[22] which he modified. He added to it a touch of Masonry culled from his summer reading in 1865, and with the assistance of the others, he began to write a constitution and to design a badge.

The other fraternities looked scornfully upon the appearance of a new secret society on campus, and members of Phi Kappa Psi became especially perturbed at Wood's use of a name, Phi Kappa Chi, so similar to their own. Consequently, some time in the early months of 1866, Phi Kappa Psi sent Harry Estill to ask Wood to change the name of the new organization.[23] To this proposal Wood consented, and on 9 April 1866, the group re-emerged as the Kappa Alpha Fraternity.[24] William Mason Bell, from Lexington, Virginia, became the first initiate after the four founders,[25] and by June 1866, six others had joined the new society.[26]

Unlike the typical chapter of the modern college fraternity, Wood's newly formed Kappa Alpha was a very serious affair. Most of the members were religious men; several were former Confederate soldiers whose outlook on life had been sobered by four years of war. "None were given to politics, baseball, or boating, the college dissipations of that day."[27] Consequently, the early members, led by Wood and William Nelson Scott, who was preparing for the ministry, immediately attributed a high ethical purpose to the new society. Although in 1866 this purpose was still vaguely defined, the early members nonetheless quickly developed a loyalty toward their newly formed fraternity.

William Nelson Scott played a part in the early founding which was second only to Wood's. As Wood lived in the country, he had few acquaintances at the college. On the other hand, Scott lived in town and came in contact with the entire college community. Thus, Scott procured most of the early members for the organization.[28]

In May 1866, an older member of another fraternity at Washington College came to Wood and strongly urged that Kappa Alpha be given up as a hopeless undertaking.[29] The new fraternity managed to survive and by Commencement 1866, several of the members were wearing badges which Wood had designed with Walsh's assistance.[30]

During the college term of 1865-1866, the enrollment of Washington College totalled only 146 students, most of whom came from Virginia and the area around Lexington. In the fall of 1866, the enrollment increased to nearly 400 students. The marked increase in enrollment can be attributed, to a large extent, to the attraction of the Lee name. From all over the South, people who still had the means to pay for a college education sent their sons to "General Lee's College."[31]

Like the other Washington College fraternities, the Kappa Alphas hoped to benefit by the increased enrollment. Seven Kappa Alphas returned to Washington College that year and looked forward to strengthening their organization.[32] Of the four founders, only William A. Walsh did not return to school.

Perhaps the most significant event in the early history of the Kappa Alpha fraternity occurred on 17 October 1866, when the society initiated Samuel Zenas Ammen of Fincastle, Virginia.[33] Although Wood had created Kappa Alpha, the task of giving substance to the small student group at Washington College yet re-

Dr. Samuel Zenas Ammen

From
The Kappa Alpha Journal
March 1898

mained. It was Ammen who gave the fraternity its particular emphasis.

Samuel Zenas Ammen served in the Confederate Army and spent the first year after the war at Botetourt Male Academy, a classical preparatory school at Fincastle, Virginia. During his three years at Washington College, from 1866 to 1869, Ammen earned a master's degree, graduating with honors and excelling in Greek and Latin. He also founded the Washington College student publication, *The Collegian*.[34]

Many years later Ammen described his initiation into Kappa Alpha:

> It was a Saturday night and dark when I went to the appointed rendezvous in the hallway of the Main Building where the two ways cross. A KA met me in a mysterious manner, seeming to rise out of the floors. He whisked me quietly out the door northward to the small building then known as the "Cat Tail." I was frightened nearly out of my wits by Stanhope Scott's gruff voice, but forgot all that speedily when confronted by the bellicose goat. A brief ride restored my equanimity, and I saw that my friend W. N. Scott was I, Thompson II, and Wood III [Chapter officers, then as now, are denoted by Roman numerals] . . . . The ritual struck me as exceedingly brief. The constitution, all of which was read to me-- was still briefer, KA being a local chapter with no thought or preparation of the great work before it.[35]

Ammen, having become a Master Mason in 1865 in Fincastle, Virginia, was accustomed to a fully developed fraternal organization with highly involved initiatory rite. He immediately recognized the shallowness of Wood's appropriated ritual and knew that the fraternity had little to offer in the realm of the esoteric to prospective members of even slight sophistication. Ammen later wrote that, "It certainly lacked all at first entrance — bare walls, bare proceedings, barrenness of purpose. It was a farce, an empty thing."[36] "Our belongings were one wooden bench for the non-official members, one sword, one minute book and one manuscript ritual."[37]

Indeed, Wood's ritual, which he had composed by merely taking large excerpts from the manuscript ritual of an old antebellum fraternity, was of a bombastic nature. It was filled with mixed metaphors and oratorical rhetoric. Very short and relatively incoherent, it lacked the drama which Ammen felt was needed to stir the imagination of the college student of the 1860s:

> First Officer (to blind-folded who is being advised not to reveal the secrets): "Let darkness, chains, and prison cells seal his infamy: his companions be prophetic shades and spectres grim!"
> Fraternity: "And ghosts and goblins, damned dire!" (Here the novice is supposed to quake.)

First Officer: "True courage shrinks not at imaginary shapes; not at horrid apparitions tall, nor ghosts that walk at night, or take their stand at new-made graves
(Sixth officer here drops a chain)
First Officer: "I hear the sound of clanking chains and uncoffined bones!"[38]

Thus, shortly after his initiation, Ammen proposed that the ritual be revised. As a result, the fraternity appointed a committee, that consisted of Wood, William Nelson Scott, and Ammen, to revise the ceremony. At first, the committee made little progress.[39]

Ammen also recommended that the fraternity refrain from initiating any more new members until the ritual had been improved. But the majority disagreed with him and, accordingly, proceeded to initiate several new members. However, shortly thereafter, Ammen's apprehensions became confirmed when five of the newly initiated men resigned their memberships several weeks before Christmas 1866.[40] They had joined to learn the mysteries of the chapter room, and when they found that they had been inducted into a young, amorphous organization without affiliated chapters, without an impressive ritual, and without social prestige, they promptly withdrew.[41] Although the fraternity immediately expelled all of them, Kappa Alpha's reputation received a damaging blow in the eyes of the student body of Washington College. Out of seven men initiated in the fall of 1866, only two remained. But the fraternity was fortunate in that one of the two remaining was Samuel Zenas Ammen. Now with the approval of the whole fraternity, Ammen immediately set to work rewriting the ritual completely, with Wood and the Scott brothers heartily agreeing with each of his proposals.

Ammen took three years to evolve the new ritual. By 1870, when Ammen had the new ceremony privately printed, Wood's original ritual had passed completely out of sight and a new theme had emerged. With the aid of speeches and essays read in chapter meeting and from his own reading in the classics and in eighteenth- and early nineteenth-century romantic literature, Samuel Zenas Ammen derived the new ceremony. He wrote the main body of the work from 1867 to 1869, during the height of Military Reconstruction. He was perplexed to see the old familiar society of the white antebellum Southerner being destroyed before his eyes. Caught in one of those times when an old civilization is dying and a new civilization is emerging, Ammen reacted to the new by seeking to preserve the values of the old. Consequently, he saw the mission of Kappa Alpha as that of conserving what he considered to be the moral values of the Old South. To articulate these values, Ammen chose the romantic concept of knighthood and chivalry, as popularized in the antebellum

South by the novels of Sir Walter Scott and others, and used it as his thematic device. As a result of his work, Kappa Alpha evolved from a small association of college students to an Order of Christian Knights, pledged to high ideals of character and honor, religious in feeling, military in organization, and committed to protect the virtue of pure womanhood. Thus, the boys who constituted the small struggling student society, could marvel at the new, lofty attributes of their organization, for within the corpus of the fraternity, Ammen had entrenched the Southern myth of chivalry.

On 17 March 1867, shortly after he had begun to rewrite the ritual, Ammen recorded in his diary:

> This society is too young, poor and weak to benefit me. Rather it injures me — does me harm in the college world. Had I entered an older society! Nevertheless, I am resolved to aid it — to try to establish it in perpetuity. It is now mine, as I made it. The members are not the best of our college world, but they are well meaning, honest, moral, gentlemanly fellows, with great kindness of feeling for me. We have among us an earnestness and energy which will overcome obstacles. After joining, I was too proud to admit my disappointment, so I stuck. Now I resolve to write my name on its history. It shall and will succeed.[42]

But just as the new ritual was beginning to evolve, President Lee dismissed James Ward Wood from school. In three terms at college, Wood had found much to occupy his time besides his studies. Early in his college career, Wood had taken to writing poetry. Using the *nom de plume* of "Ward-not-Artemus", he won a slight reputation for himself on campus as the "College Bard".[43] Wood also seems to have been much of a ladies man, and at one fraternity meeting he suggested that a Kappa Alpha chapter be established among the girls at the Ann Smith Academy where he supposedly had a sweetheart.[44]

Thus, Wood whiled away his time in writing poetry, in courtship, in establishing his fraternity, and in fanciful speculation. As a result, he constantly neglected his studies. Charles A. Graves, a student at Washington College, who roomed with Wood at Tutwiler's and who later became a law professor at the University of Virginia, described Wood's study habits:

> Wood had a good room, with wood fire, and after supper made elaborate preparations for study. He spent some time putting fresh logs on the fire, brushing up the hearth, replenishing the oil lamp, placing his table end chair exactly right, arranging pencils and pens conveniently, dusting his textbooks, putting the books needed in easy reach, end then sitting down to work, — at once dropped off to sleep.[45]

Consequently, after Wood spent three college terms of making no progress whatsoever in his studies, General Lee wrote to Wood's father, asking that he call his son home. On 25 January 1867, the fraternity gathered in the Main Building of the college to say goodbye to their founder. Following a brief farewell speech, Wood presented to the fraternity a silken KA banner that two young ladies were in the process of making for him.[46] After Wood departed on 1 February, the banner failed to materialize, for the girls' hearts had grown cold.[47]

Thus, James Ward Wood rode back up the Valley of Virginia, not to be heard from again for twenty-five years, when, in 1893, he made a brief appearance at a fraternity convention. Behind him, he left a small student organization, still very much in an embryonic state, and verging upon extinction. Although it had been his creation, its preservation, elaboration, and development fell to Ammen and others.

After the resignation and expulsion of five members in December 1866, the fraternity managed to rejuvenate itself by initiating three new members in the spring of 1867. One of the three new men was Jo Lane Stern of Richmond, Virginia. Stern, who had served as a telegraph operator in the Confederate Army, was enthusiastic and helped to breathe new life into the organization.

Members of rival fraternities sought to discredit the KAs further. After Wood departed, they charged that he, as librarian of the Washington Literary Society, had absconded with the organization's treasury. Ammen, however, proved that the discrepancy of funds came from Wood's careless bookkeeping rather than from thievery.[48] Concerned about this and other attacks by rival groups on the fraternity, Jo Lane Stern and Ammen walked down Main Street in Lexington one night in May 1867, and sat on the steps of White's Store. There, they deliberated long on the future of Kappa Alpha. They posed the question: "Shall we let the lodge die?" The fraternity was so weak at that time that, had they decided to give up, it would have disintegrated. After long consideration Stern and Ammen resolved to continue.[49]

The prospects for Kappa Alpha improved in the fall of 1867. William Nelson Scott lived at the Ann Smith Academy where his father was principal. Scott succeeded in getting Ammen a position teaching Latin and French at the Academy. At the same time, Ammen continued as a student at Washington College,[50] but boarded at the Academy. As the chapter elected him No. I (president) in the fall of 1867,[51] much of the fraternity's activity began to revolve around the girls' school. Scott had several female relatives in Lexington who began to take interest in the KAs. Scott's aunt, Mrs. Barton, agreed to make the fraternity regalia which Ammen had designed

Ann Smith Academy, The First Home of the Order
Lexington, Virginia

From
History and Catalogue of the Kappa Alpha Fraternity
Nashville, Tennessee
1891

the previous summer. Also, Scott interceded with his father and procured a room at the Academy which the fraternity furnished for its own use. Thus, by February 1868, the fraternity met in its own chapter room in full regalia.[52]

Ammen had been improving the ritual since the preceding year and one of the first times the enhanced ceremony was used was for the initiation of William Wilson Collins of Macon, Georgia, in October 1867.[53] The initiation of Collins proved extremely advantageous to the fortunes of Kappa Alpha. Collins knew John Eliphalet Hollingsworth, a cadet at the Virginia Military Institute, also from Macon, Georgia, and through Collin's persuasion, Hollingsworth joined Kappa Alpha in February 1868.[54] Immediately after Hollingsworth's initiation, Collins proposed that a chapter of Kappa Alpha be organized at the Virginia Military Institute.[55] The fraternity readily agreed to this proposal, and a month later initiated three VMI cadets who subsequently formed into Beta Chapter of the Kappa Alpha Fraternity.[56] The chapter at Washington College thereafter was designated as Alpha Chapter. Also in March, Collins, who was still fired with enthusiasm, left Lexington to form Gamma Chapter at the University of Georgia, and he remained there as a student.[57] Having been threatened with extinction only a few months before, members at Washington College now found themselves comfortably quartered in their own chapter room at the Ann Smith Academy with two new sister chapters.

Alpha Chapter was determined to exercise control over the two new chapters and any that might follow. In addition, a need arose for an officer within the mother chapter to bear the responsibility of corresponding with the new chapters and of providing them with copies of the ritual and constitution. Ammen had envisioned an authoritarian government, similar to that of the military, for the fraternity. He also felt that the Alpha Chapter should remain supreme over the other chapters, at least until they got on their feet. Consequently, members of Beta and Gamma Chapters took an oath to obey the Alpha Chapter in matters of fraternity law and policy. Following Ammen's suggestion, Alpha Chapter created the new post of Knight Commander to communicate with the new chapters, direct their activity, and provide them with rituals and constitutions. Consequently, on 1 May 1868, the chapter at Washington College elected recent initiate John Francis Rogers as the first Knight Commander.[50] Although he was titular head of the whole fraternity, Rogers as Knight Commander remained subject to the authority of the No. I of Alpha Chapter, who was, of course, Ammen himself. Thus, Rogers' job was mainly clerical.

The school year of 1867-1868 was one of repeated success for the young, but growing, fraternity. One unpleasant event, however, marred the record that year. Authorities caught William M. Sears, one of the charter members of Beta Chapter, stealing from another cadet. At a mass meeting of all cadets, officials shaved half of Sears' head, stripped him of his uniform, and forced him to leave school. Suffering in prestige from Sears's thievery and subsequent humiliation, the newly formed Beta Chapter at VMI made no attempts to increase their membership for a full year.[59]

In spite of this unsavory incident, Alpha Chapter had every right to be proud of the year's work. What had recently been a small local fraternity at Washington College had grown to three chapters; and members were making plans to establish chapters at other colleges in the South. Thus, the chapter planned a celebration for the end of the spring college term of 1868. The chapter had passed a ruling "forbidding the use of distilled liquors at KA festivals,"[60] so William Nelson Scott "was instructed to learn the price of a gallon of good wine."[61] Scott also persuaded his female relatives to prepare delicacies for the fraternity, and at 11 P.M. on 16 June 1868, Beta Chapter joined with Alpha at the Ann Smith Academy to celebrate what Ammen termed "The Convivium".[62] At the business meeting that preceded the banquet Jo Lane Stern received permission to organize a chapter at Richmond College.[63] Refreshments followed and included a gallon of wine, cakes, ice cream, nuts, French candies, oranges, lemonade, and raisins. Two of the many toasts and speeches eulogized the "virtues of pure womanhood."[64] Thus ended the spring term of 1868.

With the end of this session, the last of the founders, the two Scott brothers, departed from the chapter. William Nelson Scott had done much to provide for the material comfort of the Alpha Chapter. With his departure for theological school, the chapter no longer had the use of the Ann Smith Academy nor the assistance of Scott's female relatives.

During the summer of 1868, Samuel Zenas Ammen continued his improvements of the ritual.[65] Also, at that time William Anson Rogers, who had been initiated into Alpha Chapter in 1867, transferred to Wofford College in Spartanburg, South Carolina. In the fall of 1868, Rogers organized Delta Chapter of Kappa Alpha at his new college.[66]

With the loss of the Ann Smith Academy and genial Kappa Alpha promoter William Nelson Scott, Alpha Chapter became stagnant during the 1868-1869 college year. The chapter left minutes for only three meetings during the year and initiated no new members.

Rogers. Stewart. S. Scott. Bell.
Ammen. Kirkpatrick. Kilgour. W. Scott. Stern. Thompson.
Alpha Chapter, 1867
Washington College
Lexington, Virginia

From
The Kappa Alpha Journal
January 1897

Nonetheless, Alpha did make an effort to supervise the younger chapters. When John F. Rogers returned home at the end of the fall session, the chapter elected Samuel Zenas Ammen as Knight Commander.[67] Ammen, in his final year of college, worked for a master's degree, and he both founded and edited *The Collegian*, the Washington College student magazine. He had little time in his schedule to give to Alpha Chapter affairs.[68]

Beta Chapter at VMI, still in disgrace from the Sears incident the year before, also lay dormant during the academic year of 1868-1869.[69] No doubt the Sears affair also had a harmful effect on the prestige of Alpha Chapter and may well have been the chief reason for the inactivity of both of the Lexington chapters during the sessions of 1868-1869. Having been disgraced by brother Sears, perhaps both chapters thought it wise to remain in obscurity for a while until memories had grown dim.

Meanwhile, the fraternity continued to expand in the lower South under the stimulus of W. W. Collins at Gamma Chapter in Athens. In the fall of 1869, two Kappa Alphas from Gamma Chapter, John F. Bonnel and Herbert L. Fielden, transferred to Emory College at Oxford, Georgia, and established Epsilon Chapter of Kappa Alpha.[70]

Alpha Chapter showed a few signs of life during the college year of 1869-1870. Only three KAs returned to Washington College in the fall of 1869, but the chapter initiated four new men.[71] Even with seven members, Alpha Chapter again elected Ammen as Knight Commander. This, in spite of the fact that Ammen had graduated the previous spring and was teaching school in Kentucky when the election took place.[72]

In November 1869, Jo Lane Stern left Lexington for a few days to organize Zeta Chapter of Kappa Alpha at Randolph-Macon College in Ashland, Virginia. Four months later in March 1870, Stern, assisted by two new initiates from Zeta Chapter and James Smith Iverson of Alpha, established Eta Chapter at Richmond College.[73]

According to an old fraternity legend, General Lee gave his consent for Stern to miss classes for the purpose of organizing the chapters at Randolph-Macon and Richmond. This implied approval subsequently gave rise to a campus rumor that Lee favored Kappa Alpha and its extension.[74] Thus, many years later, when the fraternity began to honor Lee as the prototypical "Southern gentleman" there arose a tendency to claim Lee as the "Spiritual Founder of Kappa Alpha."

Although General Lee's alleged sympathy to the early fraternity is doubtful, he presumably was aware of Kappa Alpha. Jo Lane Stern

knew Lee's daughters and once when Lee was away from Lexington, Miss Mary Lee allowed Stern to ride the general's horse Traveler to run an errand.[75] Furthermore, in a letter of April 1870, Stern wrote:
> General Lee's most fascinating daughter is a regular built KA all over. She is always seen with the badge. Georgia must claim the glory of that, as our worthy Π is the owner of the property; I mean the badge, not the lady.[76]

These are the only two examples of any remote connection of Robert E. Lee with the Kappa Alpha fraternity. While president of Washington College, Lee had the reputation of remaining aloof from the student body and not fraternizing with any student. By 1870, there were nine fraternities at Washington College, and it is highly improbable that Lee showed any favoritism toward any of them. Many years afterward, Samuel Zenas Ammen repeatedly denied that Lee had any direct connection with the fraternity or had aided it in any way.[77] Still, much has been written about the tremendous influence of Lee's example upon the boys at Washington College during 1865-1870, the time of his presidency. Although there is no proof of his direct connection with the fraternity, the example of Lee's life greatly influenced the early KAs at Lexington. His life summed up the qualities of the antebellum South which the fraternity endeavored to maintain. It was this moral influence which caused the fraternity to honor Lee in later years, and which caused the leaders of the Fraternity to begin to cite Lee as the "Spiritual Founder of Kappa Alpha."

In February 1870, the members of Alpha wrote a letter to Beta Chapter and urged that the VMI chapter resume operations. As a result, Beta, assisted by Alpha, initiated three cadets and became active again.[78]

Just four months after they helped Beta, Alpha Chapter met for the last time in June 1870. In the fall of 1870 no one came back to Washington College to resume chapter activity, Moreover, General Lee died 16 October 1870. With the passing of Alpha Chapter, the center of fraternity activity moved south to Georgia and South Carolina, where Gamma Chapter at Athens and Delta Chapter at Spartanburg continued with fraternity expansion. By 1871, Beta chapter at VMI had also died. Although in years to come these two chapters in Lexington would be re-established, the work of organizing chapters in colleges and universities all over the Southern states fell to the chapters further south.

Kappa Alpha was only one of the fraternities that spread through the Southern states after the Civil War. Ammen had clothed it in a peculiarly Southern ideology that expressed the values of the white Bourbon class, an eventual reverence for the Lost Cause, the idealization of the Old South, a moral code based on the romantic notion of chivalry, an aristocratic suspicion of democracy, and the exaltation of the "Southern Gentleman" as worthy of emulation. Still, Kappa Alpha did not spread to colleges throughout the South any faster than other college fraternities. Rather, it grew as a part of the American college fraternity movement which gained increasing popularity on college campuses during the latter years of the nineteenth century. When, however, all the other colleges fraternities which were founded in the South after the Civil War eventually turned and established chapters all across the country, Kappa Alpha chose to remain in the South. A few KA chapters were eventually organized in California, the border states, New Mexico, Arizona, and even one chapter in Delaware. Still, for many years the greatest strength of the fraternity remained, by choice, in the Southern states.

On 11 July 1870, delegates from seven Kappa Alpha chapters and Knight Commander Samuel Zenas Ammen sat around a small table in a hotel room in Richmond. This session constituted the first annual Kappa Alpha Convention. Up until that time, Alpha Chapter had exercised an autocratic control over the other chapters. Yielding under pressure, Alpha had agreed to an annual convention to decide on fraternity law and policy, but had retained the right to elect the Knight Commander. As Alpha was to become extinct in the fall of 1870, this right would soon pass to Beta according to the fraternity rule on seniority of chapters. Any acts of the convention subsequently had to receive the consent of two thirds of the chapters. Thus, the convention did not exercise complete control over fraternity affairs.[79]

Prior to 1870, the southern KAs had discovered that there had existed for many years a Kappa Alpha Society in the North that had chapters at several northern colleges. Among the questions discussed by the delegates of the 1870 convention was the feasibility of union with the Northern Kappa Alpha, a question that was destined to be discussed time and time again in the years to come.[80]

Also at the 1870 convention, Ammen submitted his completed ritual and constitution for ratification. After three years' work, Ammen completed the ritual while he was teaching in Kentucky in 1869, and he had it privately printed that winter in Columbus, Kentucky.[81] This first printed ritual became known as the *Green Book of 1870*.

Having transacted the business of the convention, the delegates returned home. With a successful first convention behind it, the fraternity had passed its period of formulation in the Valley of Virginia and was entering a long period of expansion throughout the colleges of the South. By 1900, fifty chapters had been established. (See Appendix A)

The first Kappa Alpha chapters contrasted radically from modern college fraternity chapters with their full social life. The chapters of the 1860s were generally very small and they devoted their meetings to hearing essays and speeches on academic or highly moralistic topics. They held no dances or parties, and their only social activity consisted of occasional banquets, which were always stag affairs. The chief emphasis of the chapters seemed to lie in the ritualism of the initiations, a concern for high scholarship, character improvement through association, and the promulgation of fraternal regard between members. The early members tended to be religious and several of the early members of Alpha Chapter became ministers. In many ways the fraternity reflected the moralistic Calvinism of the Valley of Virginia from which it sprang.

Moreover, under the influence of Samuel Zenas Ammen, Kappa Alpha emerged as a reaction against Reconstruction. Through Ammen's leadership, the fraternity was committed to the preservation of traditional Southern values. Thus, after the delegates to the Convention of 1870 had ratified the ritual and had returned to their homes, Ammen could leave Richmond with a sense of satisfaction. While James Ward Wood had created a small fraternal society, devoted to vague ethical principles and fraternal friendship in the Valley of Virginia, Samuel Zenas Ammen had almost single-handedly rewritten the ritual and influenced fraternity affairs to mold KA into something different. Largely due to Ammen's work there would never be a union with Northern Kappa Alpha, nor would there be for many decades any chapters established in the Northeast, for Ammen had created a distinctively Southern fraternity.

*Gamma Chapter
University of Georgia
Athens, Georgia*

*From
The Kappa Alpha Journal
July 1893*

Chapter II

✢   ✢   ✢

INSTITUTIONAL AND STRUCTURAL DEVELOPMENT 1870-1897

To the small number of white Southerners who could somehow get together enough money to attend college during the lean years of Reconstruction and for many years afterward, the impoverished colleges of the South offered little in the way of quality education or broadening horizons. The ravages of war left in their wake wrecked academic facilities, burned libraries, and scattered students and faculty. The colleges that managed to re-open after the cessation of hostilities did so with little or no endowment, decimated faculties, and few students. Yet, immediately after the war, both state-supported and denominational colleges began to appear all across the South. They hawked their meager, even miserable educational wares to attract student tuition fees, which frequently comprised their only means of support. Often, the students who enrolled in these institutions had little previous training to prepare them for college work. Therefore, a goodly number of the Southern colleges operated with an overwhelming portion of their student bodies enrolled in the "academic" or high school departments. Consequently, many of the colleges were little more than prestigious high schools. This type of inferior institution proliferated throughout the South, with the result that too many of them had little or no claim to academic distinction.[1] The emphasis on high school departments caused a cheapening of admission and graduation policies and degrees from many Southern colleges only represented about one year of college work, if that much.[2]

The denominational colleges played a leading role in offering the pittance of higher education available to Southern youth in the years following the Civil War. Embroiled in sectarian controversy and disputes over Higher Criticism, the Baptist, Methodist, Presbyterian, and occasional Episcopal colleges fought a never ending battle to stay open:

> All of these institutions...were poverty stricken to a degree that the present generation can scarcely understand. This was because they drew their support from a poverty stricken and war-ruined country.... The history of all these Southern denominational colleges is a heartrending one — usually that of a strong and devout, if somewhat uncouth spirit at the head, with no money, almost no support even from his own church following and little desire for education among the flock.... [Trinity College in North Carolina] had fewer than one hundred and fifty students, a great number of whom — the sons of teachers and Confederate veterans, and novitiates for the ministry — paid no tuition; it had a president and three or four professors — each receiving a nominal salary of one thousand dollars a year, which was paid so irregularly that those were lucky who collected half the sum. The college

had no endowment, and, at this period, its entire annual revenue seldom exceeded three thousand dollars. It gave greatest emphasis to Greek, Latin, and mathematics, yet here, as with other sectarian colleges, religion ranked on a par with intellectual training, if not above it. "Revivals" took place every year as regularly as commencement, and to undergo the process known as "conversion" or "profession of faith" was even more important than to obtain "distinction" in the academic routine. Athletics cut practically no figure; in their place were the forensic performances of the two rival debating societies, where future American statesmen were trained in oratory and politics.[3]

The state supported colleges fared little better. At the end of the Civil War the campus of the University of Alabama lay in ashes. For lack of students and money, the University of North Carolina remained closed from 1870 to 1875, as did William and Mary from 1881 to 1887. Unable to open its doors from 1879 to 1883, the University of South Carolina was eventually saved by federal funds provided by the Morill Act, but these funds soon went to the newly established Clemson College.[4] Such conditions were repeated all across the South.

Yet, Northern capital, coupled with the resources of a few undepleted Southern fortunes, intervened. They provided what were then considered to be rich endowments for several new Southern Universities —Tulane, Vanderbilt, and the Johns Hopkins University. These, along with the University of Virginia, the University of the South at Sewannee, Tennessee, and perhaps a few others constituted the South's only claim to any intense activity of the mind during the remaining years of the nineteenth century.

It was into this collegiate environment that the Kappa Alpha fraternity spread as a part of the American college fraternity movement. Several new college Greek letter societies were founded in the years following the Civil War. During the latter half of the nineteenth century, these new organizations, joined by the older established chapters, spread the fraternity movement to campuses across the country. Most of the older, antebellum Northern and Western based fraternities had dissolved their southern chapters at the time of the Civil War. After the War many of the Northern fraternities were reluctant to re-enter the tenuous, newly re-opened Southern institutions, although a few of the Western fraternities did re-establish some of their Southern chapters.[5]

Consequently, because of the popularity of the college fraternity idea, and due to the lack of chapters already established, Southern students organized several fraternities of their own in the late 1860s. Alpha Tau Omega and Sigma Nu were both organized at the Virginia Military Institute in 1865 and in 1869, and Kappa Sigma and Pi

Chi Chapter
Vanderbilt University
Nashville, Tennessee

From
The Kappa Alpha Journal
July 1893

Kappa Alpha were founded at the University of Virginia in 1867 and 1868, respectively. These four, as well as several others, now defunct, joined with Kappa Alpha as the galaxy of new "Southern" fraternities. Sigma Alpha Epsilon, founded at the University of Alabama before the Civil War, Sigma Chi, Beta Theta Pi, Delta Tau Delta, and Phi Delta Theta were prominent among the other fraternities, Southern, Northern, and Western, that eventually established chapters in the South in the 1870s through the 1890s.

The impoverished conditions of the times greatly hindered the immediate spread of Kappa Alpha chapters across the South. Extension came slowly and often painfully, when newly founded chapters were forced to disband because of anti-fraternity laws, or due to the financial failure of the institutions in which they were located. After limited gains in chapter expansion during the first three years of the 1870s, fruitful chapter expansion came to a standstill. In addition, lack of communication between the scattered chapters and apathetic leadership placed the fraternity in a very tenuous position:

> From the establishment of Lambda, at the University of Virginia, in 1873, to the establishment of Sigma, at Davidson College in 1881, [sic] .... Not a single chapter was organized which is in existence today ....
>
> The affairs of the Order about this time were in somewhat of a chaotic condition. There was a government, but it was loose and not actively administered. This, however, was more a condition of the times than the fault of any individual. The chapters were few and far apart. The fraternity itself was small, its entire membership not exceeding a few hundreds. Communication between the different chapters was difficult and infrequent .... It appears probable that few members of that period ever gave the fraternity any very serious consideration or had any very definite conception of the fraternity spirit as we know it today. To a certain extent, the chapters were separate and independent clubs, all existing under the same name, but with little organic union between them.[6]

It was not until the early 1880s that chapter expansion began to proceed at a regular pace. In 1883 alone, under Knight Commander John S. Candler, nine chapters were established. By 1890, KA chapters existed in Alabama, Louisiana, Tennessee, Kentucky, North Carolina, Texas, and Missouri. During the 1890s, KA founded chapters in Mississippi, Arkansas, Maryland, the District of Columbia, West Virginia, and faraway California, as well as in several Southern states with existing chapters. By 1897, with thirty-nine chapters, Kappa Alpha could claim to be the largest fraternity in the South.[7]

The fraternity's organizational structure remained loosely organized and poorly governed for many years after its founding.

Ammen's constitution of 1870 had provided that the oldest chapter should elect the Knight Commander and exercise a ruling control over the other chapters. However, after Alpha Chapter disbanded in 1870, followed by Beta at the Virginia Military Institute in 1871, the status of senior chapter, as well as the center of fraternity activity, passed to Gamma Chapter at the University of Georgia. In spite of adverse conditions at the University, Gamma prospered and sustained a large membership.

In 1873, Gamma, as controlling chapter, elected Gamma initiate John Lunsden Hardeman from Macon, Georgia, to the post of Knight Commander. As Alpha and Beta chapters had died, Hardeman saw no reason for the autocratic rule of the senior chapter to continue under Gamma. Consequently, at the Convention of 1873 which met at Athens, Georgia, Hardeman persuaded Gamma Chapter to yield its power to the convention. Hardeman then resigned his office of Knight Commander, to be immediately re-elected by the newly empowered convention. Thus, after the "revolution of 1873", all jurisdiction in fraternity matters rested with the convention.[8]

While Knight Commander, Hardeman edited and printed the first two fraternity catalogues, issued an improved edition of the Constitution and Ritual, aided in chapter expansion, and required that the various chapters submit to him regular reports of their membership and activities.[9] Then Hardeman resigned in 1875. He was followed by a succession of obscure Knight Commanders who generally paid little attention to their duties and who neglected even to attend fraternity conventions.

The convention of 1875, during its meeting in Ashland, Virginia, created the post of Grand Historian. As a general officer, second in power to the Knight Commander, the officer was responsible for collecting materials pertaining to the history of the fraternity. However, this office remained titular for many years after its creation.[10]

The convention of 1877 elected Daniel Rowell Neal to the office of Knight Commander.[11] Struggling against the fraternity's problems and the laxness of communication within the organization, Neal conscientiously attempted to perform the duties of the position. He reinstituted the system of chapter reports, which had lapsed since Hardeman's administration, and published a new fraternity catalogue in 1878.[12] Neal chartered six chapters, four of which disbanded very soon after their founding: one never succeeded in getting established, two existed for a short time in academies of high school grade and one, Nu Prime, at the Pennsylvania College of Dental Surgery, represented the lone, abortive attempt to establish a chapter of the fraternity in the North. In later years, Neal received a great deal of criticism for allowing the two "academic" chapters to be established. At that time, however, the rules regarding the founding of new chapters were lax, and several more years passed before the fraternity learned the folly of establishing chapters in "fly by night" institutions of low quality.[13]

Perhaps the greatest accomplishment of Neal's administration as Knight Commander came in 1878. That year's convention, after first ruling that conventions thereafter would meet biennially, appointed a committee of five to instigate a regular fraternity publication.[14] Through the efforts of this committee the first issue of the *Kappa Alpha Journal* appeared in February 1879, with Richmond, Virginia as its place of publication. Previously, the various chapters had been expected to keep in contact with each other through the means of periodic letter writing. This practice was followed in a rather indifferent manner and resulted in poor communication.[15] Several of the Northern fraternities had led the field in publishing fraternity magazines such as the *Beta Theta Pi* which originated as early as 1872. Still, the *Kappa Alpha Journal* proved to be the first magazine established by a Southern fraternity.[16]

After only one year of publication, the *Journal* failed. Its editors had conceived the new organ to be a literary magazine and optimistically stated that given time it "will develop into a full fledged magazine like the *North American Review*."[17] Because of impoverished conditions of the time, any Southern magazine led a precarious existence. It therefore is not surprising that the *Kappa Alpha Journal* suspended publication due to lack of subscriptions. Also, a totally literary publication probably did not fit the needs of the organization.

The failure of the *Journal*, after the December issue of 1879, provided a final discouraging footnote to the tenuous and haphazard existence of Kappa Alpha in the 1870s. Largely operated by the collegiate membership, and lacking the widespread alumni support which it was to receive in later years, the fraternity existed, as previously indicated, as a loose alliance of independent clubs. Fraternity conventions were poorly attended and lacking in the legislation that might have strengthened the organization. Above all, the widespread physical poverty of the Reconstruction and early post-reconstruction era prevented any broad-based success that the fraternity might otherwise have achieved during the decade.

More sizable attainments were realized during the 1880s. During the term of Knight Commander John S. Candler, the convention of 1883 met in Richmond. The convention passed ambitious legislation designed to improve fraternity government. The legislation divided the Southern states into four Commandaries, each presided over by a resident Knight Visitor. The Knights Visitant were to be appointed by the Knight Commander and were to be responsible to him. Their duties included an annual visit of inspection to each chapter in their Commandary and reports to the Knight Commander of the findings of these visits. However, the Commandary system proved too impractical for the time and it was abolished by the 1885 convention. The convention of 1883 proceeded to abolish all remaining "academic" chapters in an attempt to restrict KA chapters to institutions which awarded college grade degrees. For the first time, efforts were made to get the fraternity on a firm financial footing. The convention enacted an amendment to the constitution that required each active member to pay five dollars annual dues to the Knight Commander on the first day of December of each year.[18]

The establishment of a fraternity journal on a permanent basis was perhaps the most important work of the convention of 1883. The name *Kappa Alpha Journal* was changed to *Kappa Alpha Magazine*, and the convention provided that of the five dollar annual dues collected from each active member, one dollar would go to support the *Magazine*. Thus, permanently funded for the first time, the fraternity organ could embark on its long uninterrupted history of publication, which continues to the present day.[19] In November 1883, the first issue of the *Kappa Alpha Magazine* appeared with Philip B. Hamer, of Bennettsville, South Carolina, as editor. Hamer had decided that a purely literary magazine did not fit the special needs of the fraternity and could not possibly compete with well established literary journals. Hamer edited the *Magazine* such that, unlike the defunct *Kappa Alpha Journal*, it was almost exclusively devoted to news and articles about the fraternity and the fraternity world at large.[20] Consequently, the *Magazine* began to include regular letters from each chapter, articles on early fraternity history, articles dealing with the various questions facing the organization, and only sporadic literary and poetic contributions from the pens of KAs.[21]

In 1884, the organization of alumni got underway with the formation of the Kappa Alpha State Association of South Carolina. The constitution of the association provided for an annual meeting in Columbia, and the purpose of the organization was to be primarily fraternal. As such, the South Carolina KA alumni became the first of several state organizations.[22]

The convention of 1885 that met in Nashville, was, perhaps, as important as any in the structural development of the fraternity. Previously, the financial affairs of the fraternity had been in a chaotic

The Kappa Alpha Journal

Is the official organ of the Kappa Alpha Fraternity, and will be issued bi-monthly during the collegiate year.

It is our intention to make the 15th of the month the date of our issue.

Address all communications pertaining to the business management of THE JOURNAL to

CHAS. N. BURCH,

1406 Broad Street, NASHVILLE, TENN.

$1.50 per annum, in advance; single Nos. 40 cents.

Entered at the Nashville Postoffice as Second-class Mail Matter.

6

The Kappa Alpha Journal Advertisement.

From
The Kappa Alpha Journal
July 1889

state. Chapters had been irregular in the payment of their dues to the Knight Commander. Although the convention of 1883 had raised active member dues to five dollars a year, partially to support the *Kappa Alpha Magazine*, only six issues of the *Magazine* appeared between 1883 and 1885. Lack of money, no doubt, was a contributing reason.[23]

For a viable organization to prosper and expand, it must create for itself a strong financial foundation. This is what the convention of 1885 proceeded to do when it established the general office of Grand Purser. At the convention, James Allen Williams, a member of Omega Chapter at Centre College, Danville, Kentucky, proposed the creation of the office of Grand Purser to administer the financial affairs of the fraternity, to collect dues from each chapter, and to retain 5 percent of the dues collected for expenses. Williams also proposed that the five dollar annual dues for active members be collected in fifty cent monthly allotments by the chapter pursers and be sent to the Grand Purser each month.[24] The convention elected Williams to be the first Grand Purser, and as a result of this new legislation and William's conscientious performance of his duty, the fraternity had sufficient funds for its magazine. Not only did it begin to appear with more regularity, the fraternity never again suffered for critical lack of money.[25]

The convention of 1885 transacted two other important items of business. It created a special chapter officer, Chapter Historian, to keep chapter records. Also of lasting importance, Horace Henry White of Chi Chapter, Vanderbilt University, moved that crimson and old gold be designated as the fraternity colors.[26]

In the fall of 1885, the fraternity magazine again appeared. Once again its name was the *Kappa Alpha Journal*, but it had new publishers, Chi Chapter at Vanderbilt University.[27] This was the beginning of the increasing amount of fraternity activity that centered around Chi Chapter and Nashville, Tennessee, in the late 1880s. Ever since its founding in 1883, Chi had been a wellspring of fraternity enthusiasm. During the same year that their chapter was founded, members of Chi Chapter established four new KA chapters in Tennessee, Kentucky, and Texas.[28] From 1885 to 1898, members of Chi published the *Kappa Alpha Journal*; and with the exception of 1885, 1887, 1888, and 1889, members of Chi also edited the *Journal* during that same period.[29] The convention of 1889 elected two Chi chapter alumni to office, Horace Henry White as Knight Commander and John Bell Keeble as Editor in Chief of the *Journal*. With that election, the majority of the administrative powers of the fraternity fell into the hands of alumni of the Nashville chapter.[30]

Because of the strong chapter at Vanderbilt, and because of an active group of resident alumni, Nashville became a center of KA sentiment and activity. It remained so through the 1890s.

Thorough and efficient government finally came to the fraternity in 1891, when the convention of that year called Samuel Zenas Ammen to return to the post of Knight Commander. Except for contributing occasional articles to the *Kappa Alpha Journal*, Ammen had not been very active in fraternity work after his resignation as Knight Commander in 1871. In 1870, he had moved to Baltimore to teach Latin, Greek, and Chemistry. He remained there and in 1881, he became an editorial writer for the *Baltimore Sun*, a position which he retained until his retirement in 1911. Thus, in 1891, when Ammen again assumed the duties of Knight Commander, he was middle aged and an experienced journalist.[31]

As Knight Commander from 1891 to 1897, Ammen re-established the practice of requiring the individual chapters to submit regular reports, and he instituted printed forms for their use. In 1893, he completely revised the ritual and constitution of the organization, trebling the size of the latter. It was also during this time that he designed much of the ritualistic and symbolic trappings of the fraternity: engraved charter, coat of arms, crest, fraternity flowers, flag, banners, chapter register, seal of the Knight Commander, and seal of the Grand Historian. With the assistance of Dr. William Sprigg Hamilton, who later became prominent in fraternity history, Ammen instituted yearly fraternity catalogues of members. In 1897, also with Hamilton's aid, Ammen established the *Special Messenger*, a secret, printed communication of the Knight Commander to the various chapters. During the last years of his term of office, Ammen promoted an abortive scheme to establish a Kappa Alpha Memorial Hall at Lexington, Virginia, the birthplace of the fraternity. And in 1897, Ammen wrote and published *Kappa Alpha in '97*, a small manual designed to introduce the fraternity to new members.[32] Furthermore, during his term, Ammen chartered ten chapters, thereby enlarging the boundaries of the organization into Mississippi, Arkansas, California, West Virginia, Maryland, and the District of Columbia.[33]

Yet, the task of strengthening the fraternity did not fall into Ammen's hands alone. The convention of 1891 also elected a new Grand Historian, Tazewell Taylor Hubard, who was an initiate of Beta Chapter and a lawyer in Norfolk, Virginia. Hubard became the first Grand Historian to perform his duties conscientiously. He kept fraternity records, administered the chapter reports and chapter correspondence, and issued rituals, charters, and other printed materials to the chapters. A product of the military training and discipline at VMI, Hubard kept the records of the organization with the meticulous care of a statistician. He made his most lasting contribution to Kappa Alpha by establishing the fraternity archives. In the process, he undertook a painstaking search for early printed and manuscript materials among the widely scattered active and alumni membership. While serving as Grand Historian for ten years, Hubard insisted on military obedience on the part of the active chapters in their communications with the General Officers. Thus, Hubard made a highly significant contribution by bringing efficient organization to the fraternity.[34]

John Bell Keeble, a lawyer in Nashville, Tennessee, and an alumnus of Chi Chapter at Vanderbilt, served as editor of the *Kappa Alpha Journal* from 1889 to 1896. During his tenure, Keeble elevated the fraternity publication to a standard of journalism, which, in the long history of the *Journal*, has been occasionally equaled but never surpassed. He used the pages of the *Journal* to express his own opinions and to agitate for fraternity reforms. For many years the Fraternity had maintained *sub rosa*, or rather illegal, non-university approved chapters on several Southern campuses, a standard fraternity practice of the time. As a result of Keeble's editorializing in the *Journal*, the convention of 1895 seriously curtailed the *sub rosa* chapters.[35] Because of Keeble's broad exercise of editorial freedom, it was only natural that he and a group of his supporters who were centered around Nashville would come into conflict with Samuel Zenas Ammen. Ammen and Keeble differed on several fraternity issues, *sub rosa* chapters, size of chapters, and fraternity extension being among them. Ammen maintained by fraternity law that his power as Knight Commander was almost absolute. He used the weight of his position to nullify Keeble's attempts to bring about the policies that Keeble favored as editor. What resulted was an intense power struggle between the Keeble and Ammen partisans. It erupted in 1897 as a political feud so intricate and so vicious that it will not be described here.[36] Suffice it to say that while the 1890s brought efficient government, prosperity and widespread expansion, the decade also brought the factor of politics into the Order. The resulting quarrels and bitterness continued on into the twentieth century.

But while more prosperous times contributed to strengthening the structural organization of Kappa Alpha, they also helped to usher in the beginnings of profound changes on the chapter level. These changes were not restricted only to the KAs, but rather they were widespread throughout the fraternity movement. Chief among the changes was the method of obtaining new members. During the lean

*Alpha Alpha Chapter's House
University of the South
Sewanee, Tennessee*

*From
The Kappa Alpha Journal, October
December 1891*

years of the 1870s and 1880s, KA chapters on Southern campuses generally were small and usually ranged from eight to twenty members. A typical chapter seldom initiated more than five to ten men per year, and often spent several weeks or even months of the school year in the choosing of new members. After a chapter chose or "spiked" a new man, he was immediately initiated, becoming a full member very soon after his original nomination. In the late 1880s and early 1890s, the competition between rival fraternities for new material became increasingly fierce and a custom began for each chapter to "rush" immediately after new members as soon as the new students came on campus. In many instances, the rival groups became so distrustful of each other, that each fall they lined up in bodies at the train depots of their college towns, waiting for trains carrying incoming freshmen. When the trains arrived, members of the various fraternities often "rushed" on board to drag away unsuspecting freshmen. Each group did everything in its power to see that these new men were promptly initiated before the rival groups could propose membership to them.[37]

This very colorful, if somewhat haphazard, method of soliciting new members evoked strong criticism from the fraternity press, not the least of which came of John Bell Keeble, editor of the *Kappa Alpha Journal*. Keeble argued that the growing tendency to "rush" for new members was undignified, ungentlemanly, and furthermore, that it cheapened fraternity membership and fraternal ties. He wrote further that chapters could not possibly choose loyal and compatible members in just a matter of a few days.[38] In spite of opposition, the "rush" system continued. With some refinement over the years, it prevailed and eventually necessitated a status of probational membership, which came to be known as "pledgeship".

Although Chapter life in the 1890s retained much of the seriousness and academic orientation that it had in the 1870s and 1880s, new factors that appeared on the Southern campuses exerted a decided influence on fraternity membership and fraternity life. Perhaps the most important of these new factors was the increased importance of collegiate athletics in the early 1890s:

> The whole college world has gone daft of the subject of athletics. The orator of old Philomathean, the scholar of his class, had given up the place of prominence and popularity to the pitcher of the baseball team or the left 1/2 back of the football eleven.[39]

Also, the new relative prosperity of the times allowed many chapters, which formerly might have been forced to meet in a college class rooms, to rent a suite of rooms, and to furnish them as permanent chapter halls. By 1895, most KA chapters occupied

Xi Chapter's House
Southwestern University
Georgetown, Texas

From
The Kappa Alpha Journal
November 1896

rented halls and four of them occupied rented houses. Four other KA chapters had been able to finance houses of their own, complete with chapter meeting rooms, lounging areas, and bedrooms rented out to members of the chapter.[40] With the coming of chapter halls and chapter houses, the chapters gradually began to turn away from their original religious, moral, and academic purposes to a more club-like or social existence. Although the transition did not take place fully until the twentieth century, it became prevalent in the 1890s. By 1895, fraternity life had changed sufficiently to cause Ammen, after a visit with Alpha Chapter, to lament:

> We now encounter some of the evils of prosperity: we are the "bloods" and look down on the class of men that first organized Alpha. Could [James Ward] Wood get in Alpha now? I found they are exclusive — they want style and social distinction. So of other chapters. Members who are simply intelligent, earnest, devoted have no standing unless "rich," "gamey," and have a crease down the trouser legs. This is to be select[?]
>
> With this well dressed idle set comes drinking and "jags."
>
> So of the Old Knights Templars: first pious, then powerful, then rich, and at last corrupt. It is with some grief that I see that the virtues that we aim at are forgotten, and I am an old fogey. Yet we shall remember that most of our chapters still cherish the old conceptions and judge a KA by his head and heart rather than by his coat and pants.[41]

Army of Templars Crossing a River

From
The Knights Templars by C. G. Addison
New York
1874

Chapter III

✣ ✣ ✣

THE ROMANTIC MIND OF THE K.A.O.

Samuel Zenas Ammen, Confederate soldier, editorial writer for the *Baltimore Sun*, and almost single-handed creator of the Kappa Alpha Order, its ritual and institutions, never quite recovered from the downfall of the Confederacy. As a student at Washington College in 1865-1870, he lamented the establishment of Reconstruction: "I saw the scandalous scalawags put over us at the courthouse in Lexington — a bunch of low country bunks, selected because they were disloyal unionists during the Civil War."[1] And years later, in 1895, he could still write, "I hate yankees and yankeeland with all my heart."[2] Aristocratic Episcopalian, Freemason, and conservative Southern Democrat, Ammen harbored a lifelong distrust of democracy:

> I do not believe in the democratic theory of government, and see only growing evils in its practice. I think an aristocratic or monarchial government better .... Homer had behind him ages of political experience when he said, "Let one govern."[3]

Conversant in French, German, and Greek; European traveler; and author of *Ammen's Latin Grammar for Beginners*, Ammen believed in the benefits of classical education as a means to obtain broad culture and refinement.[4] Although he valued hard work as reflected in his Calvinistic family background, Ammen was ever scornful of the "profligate materialism" of his age. He believed that education and high character were the loftiest achievements of human endeavor, that "wealth is to be sought as means to the end of comfort, education, and broad culture, but regard must be had, above all, for the intangibles, the possession of which dignifies life and gives it real value."[5] Subject to a fiery temper and somewhat autocratic in his dealings with other men, Ammen was the very embodiment of the old Southern elitism which held that only the fit and the trained should rule. Kindly, reserved, and forever dignified, Samuel Zenas Ammen yet exhibited traits at odds with the age in which he lived. If the era of the late nineteenth and early twentieth centuries can be characterized as an age of ruthless economic exploitation, glorified by the Horatio Alger story of rags to riches through hard work, Ammen stood apart. He was a creature of the earlier antebellum period, an age which articulated its ideals in terms of chivalry, honor, and the "Christian Gentleman." A Southern Bourbon in the truest sense of the word, as one who never forgave and never forgot, Ammen saw himself as an old fashioned Southern gentleman. And, as ritualist and chief ideologue of the Kappa Alpha Fraternity, he conceived the organization as a vehicle to preserve Southern sentiment and the Southern ideal of character as he understood it.[6]

Throughout the sixty-three years from his initiation into Alpha Chapter in 1866 until his death in 1929, Ammen retained a keen interest in fraternity affairs. Besides writing the ritual and constitution of the organization; repeatedly revising it in 1893, 1904, 1910, and 1921; and serving as Knight Commander from 1869 to 1871, and 1891 to 1897, Ammen contributed frequent articles to the *Kappa Alpha Journal* on a wide assortment of fraternity topics. Furthermore, he penned most of the articles on fraternity history that appeared during his lifetime in the *Journal* and in the various editions of the fraternity catalogue.[7] Forever jealously guarding his position as father-founder of the fraternity, near the end of his life Ammen filled several manuscript letter books with proofs of his overwhelming contributions. When, in the twentieth century, William Nelson Scott and other members began to cite Robert E. Lee as the real "Spiritual Founder" of the Order, Ammen maintained that he alone injected Southern values into the organization:

> Wood and the other founders only wanted to establish a fraternity. The idea of resisting yankee ideas and conserving Southern ideas — assuming a Southern character — originated later in 1867-1871 .... The founders had no purpose of Southern conservatism, I injected that into the fraternity. It led me in 1871 in Baltimore to organize a Southern Literary and Historical Society, to flood the South with Southern data, the vindication of Poe being a leading item. To vindicate and stimulate the South to self assertion — that was the idea retained from KA thinking.[8]

Indeed, Ammen's contribution was so immense that any consideration of the ideological stance of Kappa Alpha in the nineteenth century must largely be concerned with his life and writings.

However, other influences upon the "mind of KA" can be ascertained from the writings that appear within the *Kappa Alpha Journal* between 1879 and 1898. They are the works of other men of the Fraternity, many obscure and a few famous. Works of such prominent Southerners as Warren Akin Candler, Methodist bishop and president of Emory University, and Thomas Dixon, Jr., novelist, appeared in the *Journal* during this period in the form of fugitive articles on the fraternity, its purpose, and ideals. Still, men of less renown, primarily editors of the *Kappa Alpha Journal* — Horace Henry White, Walter Weidman Brown, and John Bell Keeble — provided grist for the idea mill of the organization. Other men, too numerous to name, contributed single articles to the *Journal* and expounded upon the cluster of ideas which surrounded and embodied the self conception of the fraternity, ideas which were first expressed in Ammen's ritual.

To many familiar with the purely social aspects of modern

college fraternities, the very notion that certain of these organizations in their nineteenth century form could have propounded an ideology that embraced a system of morality and philosophy, may seem a bit strange. But nineteenth-century Southern fraternalism was a very serious affair, given little, if at all, to the elaborate social life which characterizes present day Greek letter organizations. Collegiate chapters retained a small membership and met in great secrecy. Meetings primarily consisted of chapter business, initiations, literary exercises, and informal discussions of a convivial nature. And although perhaps the members of the various chapters indulged in the perennial petty vices characteristic of student life, they at least ascribed high moral and religious purposes to their fraternities and made some attempts to live up to the teachings of their secret rituals. The various secret grips, passwords, signs, and symbols were all seriously observed, and a high degree of personal loyalty seems to have existed between the members.

Accordingly, the early formulators of Kappa Alpha saw theirs as an organization embodying high ideals — moral, religious, and patriotic. As a result, they felt that the collegiate chapters existed primarily to improve the character of high minded Southern youth, by means of ritualistic teachings and through the example set by older chapter members. Yet, this moralistic as well as religious emphasis of the organization was inescapably bound up in the collective folk experience of the white South of the antebellum, Civil War, and Reconstruction periods. For Ammen and the other molders of the mentality were by no means creative in weaving genuinely original ideas into the fabric of their organization. Rather, they were reflective of the social and moral values of their own time and their own society: the middle and upper class white leadership of the postbellum South, known to historians as the Bourbons.

As has been previously stated, James Ward Wood seems only to have sought to create a college club, manifesting vague ideals and values. It remained for Samuel Zenas Ammen to mold Wood's loosely contrived apparatus into an organization with substance and a mission. For the foundations of the organization came to be contained in Ammen's ritual, which he wrote from 1866 to 1870. It is to this ritual that we now turn our attention.

Scant records survive of the early intellectual influences upon Samuel Zenas Ammen. He was born 22 October 1843, at Fincastle, in the Valley of Virginia. He was the youngest of nine children of Benjamin Ammen, a fairly prosperous manufacturer, who owned, at one time or another, a flour mill, a shoe making business, a woolen mill, and a sawmill. In 1852, Benjamin Ammen lost money on his various business interests and the family was in financial straits for the next ten years. The father, an upright Calvinist, first sent his son Samuel to a local school run by a Presbyterian minister. Later the boy enrolled in the Botetourt Male Academy, a classical school at Fincastle, where he remained until the outbreak of the Civil War. During the war Samuel Ammen served in the Confederate Army, the Confederate Navy, and as a chemist for the Confederate government. After the war he spent another year at the Botetourt Academy, and in the fall of 1866, he enrolled with advanced standing at Washington College in Lexington, Virginia.[9] As previously stated, Ammen became a member of the fledgling Kappa Alpha fraternity on 17 October 1866.[10]

To his task of rewriting the fraternity ritual, Ammen brought the influences of an ascetic Calvinist background, a classical grammar school education, exposure to the teachings of three degrees of Masonry, military service in the Confederacy, and the romantic novels of Sir Walter Scott.[11] In constructing the new ritual, Ammen garnered material from his reading and from essays presented in Alpha Chapter. But, no doubt, the most important factor that influenced his writing came from his experience as a Confederate soldier. He had seen his Cause go down in defeat and in its place erected the government of Reconstruction, that to him was a most odious alternative. Because of this experience and because he saw his own cherished Southern institutions threatened with extinction, Ammen conceived the fraternity as a vehicle to preserve what he considered to be the genius of Southern civilization — the Romantic cult of chivalry of the Old South and the ideal of the Southern gentleman:

> Such also is the explanation to be offered for the adoption by its founders at Washington College, during the session of 1865-66, immediately upon the conclusion of the greatest war of modern times, of principles, as the basis of its organization, which only that time and place could have impressed so deeply on the minds of young collegians. General R. E. Lee was President of the college. Lexington, its seat, lay in the great valley of Virginia, the scene of Stonewall Jackson's most famous campaign.... The college roll itself containing, as it did, the names of sons of Confederate officers distinguished on many a well fought field, was a reminder of great deeds, and an incitement to the cultivation of the chivalrous type of character which had made their achievement possible. Acting under the inspiration of this environment, and influenced perhaps further by the fact that one of their number had in 1861, when a mere boy, entered the army under Beauregard at Manassas, and another, having grown up on the West Virginia frontier of the Confederacy, had tasted the delights and dangers of adventurous border warfare, it is not surprising that the

founders of the Kappa Alpha established an order of Knighthood rather that an ordinary society. This reference did not, however, imply any political purpose or antipathy. The war was over, and its results acquiesced in, if not welcomed. Still it was felt that, the main object of the order being the maintenance of virtues conceived to be distinctively Southern, its prosperity would always be best secured within the limits of the Southern states.[12]

Thus, through the means of his new ritual, a Medieval knighting ceremony that contained a variant of the Chivalric Code, Ammen transformed the organization from a simple college society to a mystic Order of Christian Knighthood.

Like many antebellum Southerners, Ammen, as a youth, read Sir Walter Scott's romantic novels on knighthood and chivalry. In fact, while he was in the Confederate Army, Ammen barely escaped death when a Union shell destroyed his bed roll just a few minutes after he had left it to read one of the *Waverly* novels.[13] Just as the highly idealized writings of Scott and other writers of the Romantic movement led antebellum Southerners to see their society as a feudalistic land of chivalry, grace, and honor, these writings influenced Ammen in the belief that the Romantic code of chivalry represented the eternal values of the Old South. He believed these values to be threatened by the sharp turn of events represented by Union victory and Reconstruction. Therefore, he sought to formalize and to preserve these values in ritualistic form for future generations of Southern youth.

The values that Ammen included in the KA ritual became the definitive statement of the goals and ideals of the organization. As the document itself is esoteric, it therefore cannot be quoted. However, a discussion of the ideas it contains, by way of allusion and through the use of sources which Ammen utilized, will hopefully present the totality of Ammen's thinking without disclosing the ritualistic dialogue.

First of all, Ammen conceived of a military organization with a hierarchy of officers, presided over by a Knight Commander, who held almost unlimited authority. Likewise, each chapter was ruled by its Number I, who also had almost unlimited authority. This structure of command was entirely consistent with Ammen's monarchical theories of government, his experience in the Confederate Army, and his exalted notion of warfare as an inspiration to high character and achievement:

> There is not a little force in the saying attributed to Count Von Moltke that having in view the advantages of a people of an elevated tone of character, war is from time to time desirable for the heroic sentiments which it tends to produce. An industrial civilization has its merits, but among these cannot be reckoned an

Knights Raising Red-Cross Standard

From
The Knights Templars by C. G. Addison
Masonic Publishing Company
New York
1874

austere patriotism, carried to the point of self sacrifice for the common cause, a high sense of personal honor, fortitude under adversity, magnanimity in success, and a chivalrous regard for the weaker sex, which; though changeable with faults of its own, had always in history, as well in epic poetry supplied the world with the heroes whose large virtues it is most disposed to admire. Such at least is the claim the Kappa Alpha Order would make in defense of its semi-military type of government.[14]

Secondly, the chivalric values which Ammen wove into his ritual included a high sense of personal honor and duty, a patriotic love of home and fatherland, a paternalistic protective attitude toward inferiors, and above all, a defense of pure womanhood.

The old Southern code of chivalry which Ammen sought to preserve was based on the "great chain of being," or rather the conception of a static, hierarchical society. At the top of the chain was the upper class, the Southern planter, who fashioned himself to be a latter day aristocrat and the lord of a feudal manor, his plantation. Directly below him were the small farmers and the "po' white trash", and at the bottom of the social structure were the Negro slaves. Of course, antebellum society was much more complicated and mobile than this simple stereotype, but the important thing is that antebellum Southerners believed the stereotype. The planter, being at the top of the social pyramid, had an obligation to his peers and an obligation to his inferiors — the obligation of the nobility or *noblesse oblige* — which was embraced in the code of chivalry.

As Ammen perceived him, the chivalrous KA Knight must possess an intense sense of honor and duty. A knight's honor embraces his good name or public esteem and his keen sense of ethical conduct. The most sacred part of the knight's honor is his word or his oath. Also, it is the duty of the knight to defend his country and to protect those weaker than himself. The man who possesses this dual sense of duty and honor is considered a gentleman.

In a stratified society there are many who are dependent on the knight for protection, and it must be his obligation to protect and minister to those weaker than himself who are entrusted into his care. But this type of paternalism usually involves only ministrations to immediate needs. It does not provide for the social and economic advancement of the "weak," for they are the knight's inferiors, and he is under no obligation to aid them in such a way as to facilitate their becoming his equals. This would violate the "great chain of being", and a permanently stratified society is only right and proper. So, *noblesse oblige* is based upon the inferiority of the "weak."

Above all, the Kappa Alpha Knight is expected to guard the honor of women, which is reflective of the old Southern fetish for the protection of "pure white Southern womanhood." Man, of his own nature is base, corrupt, and given to evil sensual desires. Woman, on the other hand, is pure and angelic, although weak and frail. Man is capable of throwing off his base nature through the influence of pure womanhood. Therefore, he must worship and adore her, and protect her from all that is evil and wicked. Especially, he must guard her from attacks on her chastity, which is her most precious possession.

In a speech read before Alpha Chapter in 1868, Ammen proclaimed:

> As true knights, we mean to be faithful to God — and the ladies. ... We aim at self innoblement and protection of pure womankind — the sex whose innocence and self control inspire us to high ideals.... We are to counterwork the schemes of the seducer — to maintain the purity of the girl whom we would tempt and contaminate.... A well meaning pure woman should be scared in our eyes....
>
> The knights of a period of 500 years past, soldier monks, pledged to chastity, adoring Mary, deemed her an immaculate virgin, and taught the Western world to adore, in a measure, all pure women, as partaking of Mary's sanctity. This mystic conception of womanhood has lifted woman from her former servile status to her present position in the modern world. Chivalry has exalted her. The lady, indeed, by reason of this chivalrous regard, is treated in modern society as a superior being. Deference to her is the test of courtesy.[15]

In an article published in the *Kappa Alpha Journal* in 1892, Ammen exulted womanhood out of the realm of reality into a world of shadowy ideals:

> Why does the Kappa Alpha lover excell [sic] all other lovers the world has ever known?.... It is significant that the beau who most frequents the society of the KA sister is by no means always a lover in whom KA principles have done their noblest work. Obstrusive [sic] gallantry is the least characteristic of the seasoned brother[']s traits. The Kappa Alpha lover is seen at his best, indeed, in the studious, thoughtful retiring member, who shrinks from a too near approach to his idol, prefering [sic] to worship her from afar. It is the perfection of the sister he adores, not the transitory being who is for the moment their exponent. He reverences her for what she suggests.
>
> The qualities she exhibits in a mortal frame the KA lover detaches from her individuality and through his creative imagination sees them enlarged and idealized. Immortal youth! Angelic innocence! Celestial beauty and grace! These are the real objects of his regard, and it is these that inspire a sentiment immeasurably superior to ordinary love — a sentiment which transforms the character of the KA lover, planting him in a lofty intellectual atmosphere where debasing realism finds no admittance.... Love for him is a mute admiration, not a noisy declaration; the cult of a saint,

Pope Urban II Preaching the First Crusade.

From
The Knights Templars by C. G. Addison
Masonic Publishing Company
New York
1874

Admission of a Novice to the Vows of the Order of the Temple

From
The Knights Templars by C. G. Addison
New York
1874

maintained in an austere spirit not an earthly desire. He can love and relinquish — the noblest achievement of an exalted passion.
. . .

His sweetheart's image is his holiest of holies, but with an ingenuous diffidence he suppresses the idea of acquisition. He must protect. He must defend. He must not sieze [sic] that treasure it is his duty to guard.[16]

Idealized womanhood, idealized chivalry, and idealized honor represented only a part of Ammen's ritualistic thinking. For in addition to all of this, he included within his ritual elements of the philosophical speculations of the German Idealists, Kant and Hegel, presented in a popularized, if simplistic, form. James Ward Wood had included in his original ritual a poem, "Excelsior," by Henry Wadsworth Longfellow. On the night of Ammen's initiation in October 1866, Alpha Chapter voted to remove this poem from the ritual.[17] But Ammen used the basic ideas of the Longfellow poem in his expanded KA ritual, ideas which were derived second hand from the German Idealistic philosophers of the Romantic Movement, and were popularized by Longfellow in the poem — "The youth who bore mid snow and ice, the banner with the strange devise, Excelsior!"

The notion of Excelsior, or striving (Streben), was a basic tenet of the Romantic Movement. Man is capable of infinite perfection. The essence of life is not in the achievement, but in the constant struggle to achieve. Life is a great battle, and the true knight must forever wage battle against the corrupting forces from without, and especially, from within. Thus, the youth in the Longfellow poem sets out to climb an impossible mountain, carrying with him "that banner with the strange device." Many warn him that the mountain top is inaccessible, but onward and upward he climbs, disregarding those who would reconcile him with mediocrity. Finally he falls dead in the snow on the mountainside with his goal unreached, but "still grasping in his hand of ice, that banner with the strange device, Excelsior!"

The mountain, of course, is the struggle of life, and the impossible summit is perfection, the Ideal, which is impossible to reach. Nonetheless, the true knight must continue to struggle for it. And what is the Ideal? The Ideal is man's mental conceptualization of the perfect life. And basic to German Idealism is the idea that this mental conceptualization of the Ideal, these mental categories, have a reality of their own, and are, in fact, more real than concrete matter. The categories of the mind are superior to matter because they are perfect, while things material are always imperfect. For in his mind, man recognizes the Ideal, that which is really real, and through the use of his mind, man works to reconcile his imperfect body, governed as it is by base passions, to the Ideal. And it is through this work that man shall conquer (*Vergil*). Also, because mind is superior to matter, a life spent pursuing the Ideal, which to Ammen would mean moral and intellectual improvement, is far more important than the pursuit of the material wealth or ill gotten gain. Thus, the KA Knight is to strive for a perfect life and a perfect fraternity, and deviation from that path will lead to stagnation and decay.[18]

Consistent with its cloak of Romantic Idealism, Ammen's ritual also contained religious overtones and a theological stance expressing a variety of Christian Humanism that was akin to nineteenth-century Southern Protestantism. Thus, man is not born to a life of sin and corruption, and damned but only for the redeeming Grace of God, as in orthodox theology. Rather, man is capable of infinite self improvement; and he is given free will to choose between a clearly recognizable good and evil. By continually reconciling himself to the Ideal, he becomes daily "more like his maker," the Great Ideal, who is God. This is justification or redemption by works. And within Ammen's ceremony, as well as in the rituals of many fraternal societies, there is an ethical conversion. After repenting of his past evil deeds the novice enters into a new life in Christ and in the fraternity. His sins are forgiven, and now he must begin the difficult journey, onward and upward, to perfection and to the Ideal.

Also, Ammen incorporated another religious theme — Death and the Last Judgment. The novice is warned of that day when he shall stand in terror before the wrathful God, naked and with his sins exposed, to be judged as to whether the charitable acts of his life outweigh those which are evil and wicked. If it is found that his life has been acceptable, he may enter into the Immortality of the Soul. For if mind is superior to matter, then finite matter will eventually fall away. The material body will die and turn to dust, but the Soul, the mind, that part of man which more nearly approximates the Ideal will live on forever.[19]

Concerning morality, Ammen believed that the real is rational. Thus, moral values are absolute and easily discernible among rational men. All life is a conflict between good and evil, light and darkness. This conflict is within the world and within each man. Life begins with innocence, but youthful innocence knows no evil. Thus, innocence provides no means for defense and is unable to resist attack. So, innocence is eventually corrupted by vices. From corrupted innocence, man must turn to virtue. For virtue, although conscious of defilement, is yet strong by experience. We admire innocence, but virtue alone is practical. For innocence is weak in the presence of vice, and to approach the Ideal, man must know all evil, yet prefer what is pure and virtuous.[20]

And how can man strengthen himself to follow the path of virtue and to strive toward the Ideal? According to Ammen, man must develop his mind through the discipline derived through academic endeavor in order to subjugate bodily passions:

> Primitive man was little superior to the brute, but education will lift us up to the skies. By exercizing and strengthening the intellect it puts the reins of government in the hands of reason and frees us from the domination of the passions. What is gross, earthy, sensual in us is brought under. Life attains serenity and security only as its vista is widened which balances and corrects our judgments.[21]

Thus, the path of virtue and the development of character lies partly in mental discipline and the acquisition of knowledge. For again, mind is superior to matter, and the evil of the material world may only be overcome by the developed intellect.

But the formulation of character and the upward path to the Ideal is facilitated by another important factor — the association of men of the highest character. And thus is provided the *raison d'être* of the fraternity — the selective banding together of young men of the highest type for the mutual improvement of all. For character improvement to a large degree comes through association. Although Ammen originally expressed this idea, it was expanded later by other KAs, notably John Bell Keeble, editor of the *Kappa Alpha Journal* from 1889 to 1896:

> Fraternities are great fashioners of character. Emerging from the careful influences of home, the youth of 18 comes in to the bounds of college life, and standing upon this elevation views manhood, the longed for possession, the land of promise. There are times in the working of iron when it is pliable and soft. Almost a liquid, it is easily moulded into any shape. As is the mould, as wills the moulder, so will the cold iron be. Either as a thing of use, or unshapen and useless, cast aside. At this period their character has gone through the preliminary processes, and is ready to be shaped and fashioned in the years now at hand.
>
> Nothing has so great an influence on a young man as association. Show me a man's best friends, and knowing these, I can easily estimate the man himself.[22]

To achieve the goal of mutual upliftment through the association of men of high character, and to achieve the goal of a close brotherhood, the fraternity must be selective. Thus, from the very beginning, a unanimous vote by secret ballot was required before any man could be elected into membership.[23] For the early KAs all agreed upon the necessity of a homogeneous membership:

> ... we deem it proper to take in only certain classes of young men, since to take in persons of every disposition and character would

frustrate the objects we have in view. We seek to obtain persons either with characters already formed, and who show a tendency to make use of the talents which God has given them, or else we take those with characters not yet fully developed, and in this plastic form, we hope to mould and fashion them for true and noble manhood. We do not like to take a leap in the dark; hence, we do not always take a man on his first entering college. When a stranger comes to college, we make it a point to seek his acquaintance, try to assist him, and if he seems to be worthy, we then take steps towards bringing him into our order.[24]

Yet, early spokesmen differed slightly in regard to what were to be the qualifications for membership. While all agreed that the candidate for membership should, above all, possess the qualities of a gentleman, and while the poverty of the times prevented wealth from ever being a serious consideration, KAs disagreed as to whether prominent family background and social rank should be a prime consideration in choosing new members. On this question KAs divided along a traditional aristocratic/democratic line. While some argued that family background, social acceptability, and college popularity were the prime considerations in the choice of new members, others lampooned aristocratic pretensions:

> The average American is inflicted with fundamental pain by all this snobbish cant about "aristocratic exclusive-ness," "ancestral privilege," and such like business ... This land is too youthful to admit of an indisputable aristocracy, and too democratic to allow any exaggerated, impassioned attachment to ancestral portraits and armorial trappings.[25]

John Bell Keeble, in many articles concerning qualifications for membership, took a middle course in describing the ideal candidate:

> KA's know that clothes and manners do not make a gentleman [any] more than harness makes the horse.... We want no snobs in KA. We want no "rakes," no debaunchers [sic], however blue their blood. We want no reflection of the light of past generations. We want men who can give light, men who are worthy and able to transmit nobleness of character, thought, and achievement to coming generations .... Do not understand that we inveigh against family and birth, we do not. We would agree with the autocrat of the breakfast table in this regard, who in substance says, Everything being equal give us the man with family portraits and pride; — but we do inveigh against the policy of making this the sole requisite to receiving a passport into the order.[26]

Yet Keeble's position fell short of egalitarianism:

> Though egalitarianism may be the coming thing, we do not think that now. Fraternities [of the future] will be homogenous and representative of various social groups.[27]

The aristocratic versus democratic cleavage in regard to the solicitation of new members was not often discussed among fraternity leaders, nor did it seem to go very deep. It was only indicative of a Southern white society which often strangely saw itself as elitist and democratic at the same time. While few leaders seemed to follow the monarchical theories of Ammen, most of them reflected a tenuously contrived democracy that was often perforated by a measure of elitism. Their ideal of the Southern gentleman was often tinged with considerations of class.

It is important to note that once these ideas, embracing the moral, religious, and social values of the fraternity, were schematized into Ammen's ritual, they were never seriously challenged or questioned. Rather, they passed from generation to generation of fraternity members as absolute entities, and as the eternal ideals and principles of the Fraternity. Ammen was conscious of this as he wrote into his college journal in February 1868:

> It is queer to me to see men swearing to observe my ideas which are about to be carried over the whole South. Here and elsewhere forever my teachings will be perpetuated.[28]

The teachings of Ammen were indeed perpetuated by Keeble and others who wrote articles elaborating upon them. These articles appeared frequently in the *Kappa Alpha Journal*, where they went unchallenged. No one even seriously called them into question. For among the loyal KAs, Ammen's text became sacred — as is the tendency regarding the esoteric ceremonies of secret societies. And as the late nineteenth century was hospitable to absolute moral and social values, KAs of that period seemed to greet their fraternal teachings, couched as they were in mystic symbol and sign, with a non-reflective acceptance and with a sense of reverence.

Any attempts to ascertain the universality of acceptance of Ammen's ideas among the general membership would be almost impossible. For, at any given time, only a handful of alumni leaders of the fraternity ever regularly wrote upon fraternity matters. However, one indication of the sentiments of the general membership remains the new chapter letters carried in every issue of the *Kappa Alpha Journal*. Each chapter was expected to contribute letters outlining chapter news to every issue of the *Journal*. These letters, which usually were written in the sophomoric, bombastic prose that was so characteristic of the nineteenth century, generally reflected an exuberant faith in the teachings of the fraternity. Likewise, the random remaining minute books of the individual chapters also reflect a seriousness of purpose and a devotion to fraternal ideals — Ammen's ideals.

Whether or not these values were steadfastly held among the majority of the membership, or whether they only represented the official rhetoric through which a college club justified its existence, can also never be known with certainty. Many institutions seem to evolve a rather impressive set of principles to justify to themselves and to the world that they exist for a purpose more noble, and more sublime, than the rather simple purpose for which they were founded — the facilitation of human friendship and social enjoyment.

However, there can be little question that the men who continued to work for the fraternity throughout their adult lives held the teachings of the organization with great reverence. Both the public and private writings of the General Officers resonate with a deeply held zeal for the purposes of the fraternity. Perhaps an apt description of their affection can be found in a word which they used often in their writings — sentiment. The loyal KAs exhibited an intense feeling toward their fraternity, a sentimental attachment which evidenced itself in the bonds of fraternal friendship which they believed to exist between each other and in the rapturous flights of prose which they often utilized to describe their beloved Kappa Alpha:

> I once heard a distinguished Kappa Alpha say that but three books are needed for the formation of a perfect man — Shakespeare, the Bible, and the Kappa Alpha Ritual. Shakespeare, he proceeded to explain, imparts general culture, the Bible forms the Christian, but the KA Ritual creates the chivalrous Christian gentleman, the noblest product of the civilization of the world's most enlightened age.[29]

Samuel Zenas Ammen, as well as the other nineteenth-century formulators of Kappa Alpha, conceived the organization to be, first and foremost, a moral force for the intellectual and ethical upliftment of the membership. And, in seeking a model from which to derive KA ideas of ideal manhood, Ammen utilized the image closest to his own experience, the old Southern ideal of the Christian gentleman. In doing so, and by formalizing that image in a secret ritual, Ammen aided in the portage of the social and moral ideals of the Old South into subsequent generations. Thus, the KAs carried with them through the nineteenth century and into the twentieth, the mythic values of a former age.

Chapter IV

✧   ✧   ✧

THE PHANTOM OF NORTHERN EXTENSION

The one characteristic that sets Kappa Alpha Order apart from all other college fraternities is its peculiar affinity for the entire mystique of "Southernism." For generations into the twentieth century the KAs extolled the virtues of the "Southern gentleman," venerated the Lost Cause, and paid homage to Robert E. Lee as the archetypal example of an ideal life. Prominently displayed Confederate flags on the portals of almost every house and yearly costume balls have paid tribute to a romantic conception of the Old South and the Confederacy. Not a few residents of sleepy Southern college towns in the past were annually awakened by the sound of cannons and accompanying rebel yells, violating the night time stillness, and a host of KA songs glorify the Southern origins of the fraternity:

> In Eighteen-hundred and sixty-five
> At Washington and Lee,
> There was a band of soldier boys
> As brave as they could be.
> They followed Lee and Jackson
> From the mountain to the bay,
> And they said we'll get together
> And we'll call ourselves KA.[1]

Samuel Zenas Ammen explained the distinctively Southern slant of Kappa Alpha as having greatly depended upon the post-war conditions at Washington College in Lexington, Virginia, where the fraternity was founded. In "The Kappa Alpha Fraternity," in the 1922 edition of the *Directory of the Alpha Order*, Ammen wrote that "the character and special aims of the Kappa Alpha Fraternity are in some degree due to the personality of its creators, but in a great degree to the time and place of its origin."[2] He then proceeded to demonstrate how the cruelty of the invading Yankee army, the bitterness of Confederate defeat, and the excesses of Radical Reconstruction government encouraged the original KAs at Washington College to mold their organization to "promote a moral and intellectual propaganda for the protection of Southern civilization."[3]

Yet, there were other fraternities founded about the same time in almost identical situations, that for a time remained in the South and retained a membership and sentiment strictly Southern. Still, all of these Greek letter organizations, which comprised the nineteenth-century galaxy of Southern fraternities — Alpha Tau Omega, Sigma Nu, Kappa Sigma, and Pi Kappa Alpha — eventually transcended sectional considerations, established chapters in colleges all over the country, and became truly national fraternities. Only Kappa Alpha remained Southern, and except for a small group of chapters in the far West, the KA active chapters remained for decades within the boundaries of the old slave states.

Consequently, although the conditions surrounding the founding of the fraternity were important in giving it its characteristic Southern bias, it was the particular beliefs of the leaders of the organization and of a goodly portion of the membership that worked to keep Kappa Alpha in the South from almost the very beginning. The story of how KA was kept Southern is best understood when told in its entirety.

As noted previously, poverty severely limited fraternity expansion for many years after the Civil War. Chapters only existed in Virginia, South Carolina, and Georgia until 1880, when the first chapter was established in North Carolina. And it was not until three years later, in 1883 and eighteen years after the founding of the fraternity, that chapters were finally established in Tennessee, Alabama, Kentucky, and Texas. Expansion moved slowly, and KA chapters were not planted in some Southern states until the first decade of the twentieth century.[4] Yet, after 1883, chapter expansion moved at a regular pace, and by 1897, thirty-nine chapters were in operation.[5]

It was in the early years of limited expansion, the 1870s and early 1880s, that the opportunity first presented itself for the fraternity to expand into the old Northeast. KA's expansion across the Mason-Dixon line would have occurred by uniting with the oldest social Greek letter organization in America, Kappa Alpha Society. The society, which had been founded at Union College, Schenectady, New York in 1825, maintained four chapters in New England and New York State in the 1870s and 1880s.[6] Because this Northern organization bore a similar name, the two Greek letters KA, early attempts were made to unite the two fraternities. The story of the flirtations between Kappa Alpha Society and Kappa Alpha Order is veiled in legend, part of which continues to this day.

Before the Civil War, a chapter of Kappa Alpha Society had existed at the University of Virginia. At the outbreak of hostilities in 1861, this chapter of Northern KA disbanded, both because of the war and because many of its members left college to join the Confederate Army. However, at the time it disbanded, members of this group allegedly left a copy of the Kappa Alpha Society ritual, bound up in wrapping paper, with the librarian at Charlottesville with the understanding that it would remain sealed in the library for the duration of the war. Members of Northern KA expected to return after the war, reclaim the ritual, and reestablish the University of Virginia chapter. But the chapter was never re-established, and no one returned for the ritual for several years after the war.[7]

After the Southern KA's original founder, James Ward Wood, departed from school, speculation grew within the old Alpha Chapter at Washington College about the source of Wood's original ritual and how he had arrived at the name KA. The story about the Northern Kappa Alpha ritual at the library in Charlottesville reached Lexington. Some of the members of the old Alpha assumed that Wood had managed to obtain this same ritual, and that he used it as the basis of both his original ritual and the Greek name Kappa Alpha.[8]

The fact that this story is probably untrue makes little difference.[9] What is important is that, in the early 1870s, after the early founders had ceased active participation in the fraternity, the story persisted. It led many to believe that there might be a connection between the two Kappa Alphas. As early as the first convention of 1870, discussions arose about establishing Northern chapters and about uniting with Northern KA.[10] And at the fourth convention in 1873, a committee was appointed to:

> ... confer with a Kappa Alpha Fraternity having chapters in Massachusetts and New York with a view of learning if the two were related, and, if so, whether a union between the two would be desirable, and if desirable, if such a union would be expedient.[11]

This committee made its report at the fifth annual convention of 1875. It had found that there was no connection between the two fraternities, and the committee report caused the convention to pass a resolution stating that the convention did not seek union with Northern Kappa Alpha, and furthermore,

> ... that we glory in our Southern origin, and while we would not object to seeing our fraternity spread northward, still this must be done by the extension of our own branches, and not by ingrafting [sic] our young scion into a Northern stock where the principles of Southern chivalry and Southern manhood shall be blighted forever.[12]

Seemingly this resolution would have settled the matter once and for all, but as the active supporters of the fraternity in these early years were collegiate members, and as the whole collegiate population changed every few years, the question of union with Northern Kappa Alpha was destined to come up again. When it reached the floor of the convention of 1879, the assembled body again voted down the measure.[13] Still later, at the convention of 1883, a committee reported in favor of uniting with Northern KA, providing that the union did not force any compromise in fraternity principles, the Convention took quite different steps. The Convention authorized the appointment of a committee to investigate and report to the chapters as to whether and upon what conditions would Northern KA unite.[14]

The surprisingly open attitude of this convention toward union evoked discussion on the subject during 1884 in the newly reestablished *Kappa Alpha Magazine*. However, only one article appeared favoring union. James W. Morris, of Lambda Chapter at the University of Virginia, argued that Northern KA desired union and that they had approached Southern KA twice on the matter. He pointed out that union would increase the size, prestige, and wealth of Southern Kappa Alpha. Also, according to Morris, a union could be consummated without any loss of fraternity principles, for he proposed a simple joining together of secrets and ceremonies of the two fraternities. In reply to former and anticipated arguments against union taken from a sectional viewpoint, Morris pleaded:

> I trust we have passed the stage where the North is our bitter enemy, that we have passed the border line of blood, that we have "risen above the clouds of partisanship and breathe the air of liberal citizenship." We are young men, full of all the enthusiasm and generous patriotism of youth accepting the results of our great contest, nobly fought and nobly lost we are again citizens of one great country bound by the ties of common government... Such an objection is chimerical and unworthy of our liberal considerations.[15]

Morris concluded by stating that because of its small size, Northern Kappa Alpha would never be able to control the proposed united fraternity.[16]

However, Morris' attempts to bridge the bloody chasm were of little avail. A quick succession of articles followed his in the *Kappa Alpha Magazine*, all of them disclaiming the proposed union. Warren Akin Candler, later famous Methodist bishop and president of Emory University, propounded the argument that union with Northern KA would be a measure of great folly. For if Southern KA were a mere clique of college clubs, then such a union would be permissible; but if, in fact, the fraternity was pledged to uphold certain great principles, then a union could not be effected unless both groups shared the same principles. Candler went on to say that the fraternity might as well unite with Sigma Alpha Epsilon, the Masons, or the Odd Fellows, than with some unknown Northern group that just happened to share the letters "KA". He disparaged those who would sacrifice the principles of the fraternity for Northern prestige and money.[17] In another article, R. L. M. Parks of Epsilon Chapter expressed similar fears. In addition, Parks replied to Morris on the sectional issue by stating what was perhaps the main reason why the two fraternities would never unite:

> I agree with him [Morris], that the bloody chasm has been bridged to some extent; but at the same time there is far down in every

Southern man's heart a feeling which cannot be overcome; in every mind a recollection of roaring cannon and rattling shell which cannot be effaced. There could never be that quickening of the pulse, that flushing of the cheek, and that bounding of the heart, that every K. A. now feels when he meets another. We need the assistance of nobody, we ask the assistance of none. Let every "Knight of the Crimson Cross" do his duty and K. A. will be able to take her stand in the foremost rank of Greek fraternities. Let us bear aloft the banner with the strange devise "Excelsior:" "let Southern breezes kiss it, let Southern skies reflect it," Southern K. A.s love it, and Southern K. A.s will work for it.[18]

In the same issue of the *Kappa Alpha Magazine* Samuel Zenas Ammen wrote one of the first articles on fraternity history to be written. In it Ammen pointed out that, in spite of what was previously supposed, there was no original connection between the two fraternities. Furthermore, a union of the two would sacrifice "the perfect cordiality of sentiment at present existing between the members of our order."[19]

But Northern Kappa Alpha itself levied the final blow to the scheme of union between the two groups. In two letters, one from the chapter of Kappa Alpha Society at Williams College to the chapter of Kappa Alpha Order at Davidson College, and the other from the Northern KA Chapter at Cornell University to James W. Morris, the Northern fraternity squelched any hope of union. The letters stated that Kappa Alpha Society was satisfied with its position in the North and with its four chapters. The letter to Morris went further in expressing a fear that Southern KA would "swallow up" the Northern society, due to the small size of the latter, that "revered traditions" had, no doubt, grown up in both societies which could not be reconciled, and that little advantage could come from the union of two groups with nothing in common but two Greek initials.[20] With this, the whole matter was dropped.

Although the poorly supported plan of union with Northern Kappa Alpha failed, Southern KA had another alternative by which it could have become a truly nationwide fraternity — the northern extension of its own chapters, an alternative which it repeatedly chose not to take.

In the early 1880s, the post-war, Southern-born fraternities began establishing chapters in the Northern states. In 1881, Alpha Tau Omega took the lead by establishing a chapter at the University of Pennsylvania and quickly followed it with several other Northern chapters. Kappa Sigma founded a chapter at Lake Forest University in 1880, which was soon killed by anti-fraternity laws, but a firm foothold in the North was attained when a chapter was established at Purdue University in 1885. Sigma Alpha Epsilon established its first Northern chapter at Penn College, Gettysburg, Pennsylvania, in 1883, and Sigma Nu entered the University of Kansas in 1884. Pi Kappa Alpha remained strictly a Southern fraternity until the twentieth century. Its convention of 1889 restricted extension to the Southern states in order to permit concentrated development. This restriction was not removed until 1909. Once that occurred, Pi Kappa Alpha founded a chapter at the University of Cincinnati in 1910.[21]

Ironically, Kappa Alpha Order was the first Southern-born fraternity to attempt to establish a chapter in the North. In 1877, J. H. Campbell, a transfer from Beta Chapter, who was attending the Pennsylvania College of Dental Surgery in Philadelphia, secured a charter from D. R. Neal, Knight Commander, to establish a KA Chapter at that institution. Four men were initiated, but the chapter died when the last of the four graduated in 1879.[22] Also, in 1880, Kappa Alpha made an unsuccessful attempt was made to establish a chapter at Marietta College. Located in Marietta, Ohio, the college was just across the river from Parkersburg, West Virginia, the home of D. R. Neal, then Knight Commander.[23]

These two attempts seem to have been the only times that Kappa Alpha tried to enter the Northeast. Yet, the question of Northern extension continued to be discussed at KA conventions, in the *Kappa Alpha Journal*, and within fraternity circles for many years afterward. Although the vocal advocates of Northern extension were at all times sporadic and few in number, their recurring persistence in demanding that the fraternity should establish Northern chapters caused the conservative leaders of the fraternity to rely continually on pro-Southern apologetics. These, in turn, intensified the already recognizable Southern slant of the organization. By choosing to desist in establishing chapters in the North, the KAs became aware of themselves, not as a Southern fraternity, but as "The Southern Fraternity."[24] Thus, the abortive Northern extension movement was significant in that it contributed heavily to the unfolding self-image of the organization.

Yet, the KAs gradually broadened the limits of their chosen "Southern" domain to include first the border states and eventually the far West. The first successful attempt to establish chapters outside the boundaries of the old Confederacy came in 1887 with the founding of Alpha-Delta Chapter at William Jewell College in Liberty, Missouri. In the seven years that followed, KAs established chapters in the border states of Missouri, Kentucky, West Virginia, and Maryland, as well as in the District of Columbia. Among these were Alpha-Lambda at the Johns Hopkins University, founded by Samuel Zenas Ammen in 1891, and Alpha-Nu at the Columbian

Alpha Delta Chapter
William Jewell College
Liberty, Missouri

From
The Kappa Alpha Journal
Mid-Summer
1894

University [now George Washington University] in Washington, D.C., which was established in 1894.[25]

During the 1880s, the discussion of Northern extension had been of an occasional nature, but in the wake of the founding of new chapters in the border states, articles dealing with the subject began to appear with increasing frequency within the pages of the *Kappa Alpha Journal*. The Richmond convention of 1893 voted down a motion to consider Northern extension, but the idea continued to have its advocates.[26] After Samuel Zenas Ammen, Knight Commander, chartered a KA chapter at the University of California at Berkeley in early 1895, the question apparently gained renewed interest.[27] A few months later at the Atlanta convention of 1895, several fraternity luminaries staged a formal debate on the topic. John Temple Graves, noted Southern orator, and Clark Howell, editor of the *Atlanta Constitution,* took the affirmative while Samuel Zenas Ammen, Knight Commander, and John Bell Keeble, editor of the *Kappa Alpha Journal*, took the negative. The convention made no decision on the matter.[28] For many years afterward the debate over Northern extension continued within fraternity circles, but by 1895 the lines had been clearly drawn, and subsequent discussions on the subject merely repeated the same arguments.

Among the ranks of those who opposed Northern extension, none was more vocal than Samuel Zenas Ammen. In article after article in the *Kappa Alpha Journal* and over a period of many years, Ammen repeatedly defended the unwritten fraternity policy of restricting chapters to states encompassed in a broad definition of the "South." He argued against Northern extension on several grounds and fully utilized the weight of his position as founder and author of the ritual to substantiate his arguments. First of all, Ammen argued that KA chapters in the North would be corrupted by the influence of other Northern fraternities, which he considered to be little more than fashionable drinking clubs, lacking the high ethical purpose of fraternities in the South. Secondly, he pointed to the limited success that other Southern fraternities had achieved while competing with wealthy Northern fraternities. Thirdly, Ammen expressed the fear that if chapters were established in the North, wealthier Northern members might dominate the *Kappa Alpha Journal* and the fraternity convention. Fourthly, he expressed a reluctance in believing that Northern and Southern men could genuinely greet each other as brothers, believing that fraternal feeling could only arise among those of a similar background and tradition. And finally, Ammen repeatedly insisted that the Kappa Alpha fraternity had been established primarily to preserve Southern ideals of character and gentlemanly conduct, and that these ideals could only be preserved among men of Southern birth and sympathies.[29]

This final argument emerged full grown in Ammen's Knight Commander's report to the 1895 convention:

> The steady adherence of the Order through thirty years to a definite policy of keeping to the South was not an accident but was due to a conviction that our initial aim is different from that of other fraternities, and the older members cannot but regard the proposal of Northern extension as a proposal to abandon our distinctive aim and assimulate [sic] ourselves to other fraternities which lack our special mission.
>
> But I do not believe that we have outlived the principles, the sentiments, the aspirations which animated past generations of Kappa Alphas. The fundamental teaching of the Order has been that we should cherish the Southern ideal of character — that of the chivalrous warrior of Christ — the knight who loves God and country, honors pure womanhood, practices courtesy and magnimity [sic] of spirit, and prefers self respect to ill-gotten wealth. This ideal of manhood was threatened, in the opinion of our founders, by the recent triumph of another people of a mixed race, having a different history and inspired by different ideals. The Order was to be a shield for its protection. The sphere of its operations was accordingly conceived to be in the South exclusively. The idea of going North was not entertained, but was rejected as inconsistent with their object which was to conserve what was distinctive and best in Southern character.
>
> This conception of our mission, retained from 1865 to 1895, accounts for the unvarying resolution of the Order to remain in the South. There are no politics in it; none whatever. We have received into our ranks men of all parties and from all sections of the country, prescribing, in effect, but one condition, namely that Southern ideals, as realized in the history of the South in the acts of its great men, be regarded — I will not say with partiality — but with sympathy, and not with antipathy . . . .
>
> Northern extension means either going North to impress Southern ideals on Northern youth, or it means the abandonment of our distinctive aims . . . .
>
> In staying South . . . KA has secured homogeneity of membership, the first condition of true fraternal spirit and the only real bond of unity and peace. Hence our success and cordial regard. . . .
>
> For a parallel in our case let us imagine the *KA Journal* edited in Kansas or Massachusetts, and in the leading article a discussion of John Brown, the "martyr," or of the "rebellion". But before this result has been reached all fervor of KA feeling will have gone out of our Southern KA's, and you and I will have repudiated membership in a fraternity so perverted and degraded.[30]

Ammen's repeated appeals to latent Southern nationalism effectively achieved his purpose. For the fraternity, by and large, remained in the Southern and border states. Ammen himself, as Knight Commander, chartered two chapters in California in 1895. However, he did so with great reluctance, and then only after rationalizing to himself that enough Southern "sentiment and men from the South existed in California to warrant the western move," and that, in fact, California could be considered sort of a Southern State if the Mason Dixon line were to be extended across the country.[31]

Evidently a large majority of KAs supported Ammen's insistence on keeping the fraternity in the South. Among them was another Southern sectionalist, Horace Henry White, who served as Knight Commander immediately before Ammen, from 1889 to 1891. White commented in a letter in which he turned over the reins of the fraternity to Ammen:

> During my whole time of my connection with the Order, as Editor, Grand Historian, and Knight Commander, and as delegate to most conventions since 1883, having a wide personal acquaintance in the Order, I have found the Order to be intensely Southern and democratic — Repeatedly [sic] decided not to leave Southern territory. I refused a charter to the University of Kansas, because sentiment there was Northern. Ours is an Order of Southern gentlemen in our view.[32]

Yet a slightly more moderate view was taken by John Bell Keeble, who served as editor of the *Kappa Alpha Journal* from 1889 to 1896. Keeble believed that KA chapters in the North would have extreme difficulty in competing with the numerous and well established Northern fraternities, and he cited the fact that other Southern fraternities which had gone North had, at first, suffered extreme difficulty in doing so. Keeble also believed that Northern extension would sacrifice the concord and homogeneity enjoyed among Southern KAs. Still, Keeble was sensitive to the attacks made by editors of other fraternity magazines, that KA's reluctance to leave the South was due to prejudice and sectional bitterness.[33] And, thus, he sought to justify the Southern policy of the fraternity on other grounds. Keeble applauded the entrance of KA into the California schools and came to favor Western extension in lieu of Northern extension:

> ... it is clearly established that KA has no part in the sectional bitterness which has long been attributed to its membership.... The entrance of the fraternity into California is positive proof of the sentiment of the fraternity on sectionalism. California is essentially a Northern state. When the University of California was entered the old doctrine was discarded, now Stanford. That it is wise to enter the West, we do not hesitate to affirm. All bridges are burnt away; we cannot now go back.[34]

Keeble also privately attacked Ammen's obvious sectionalism, resulting in the widening of an already present rift between the two fraternity leaders.[35] In his last editorial as editor of the *Journal*, Keeble wrote:

> I am opposed to the fostering of any sectional feeling in the breast of young men. The day for that is asleep in the grave, with the stone of two decades upon it.[36]

But Keeble represented the voice of a tiny minority, for Ammen's sectionalism prevailed within the fraternity. Likewise, the promoters of Northern extension, representing a small, unorganized group of KAs, were destined never to achieve their goal. Of their number, only John Temple Graves and Clark Howell spoke with the authority of prominence. The rest of them, mainly a few active members in the various chapters, contributed occasional articles to the *Kappa Alpha Journal* arguing for the benefits of a nationwide organization. Their voices were too weak to challenge seriously the voice of Ammen and the sentiments of the majority whom he represented. Even into the early years of the twentieth century, articles occasionally appeared in the *Journal* favoring Northern extension. Each of them was promptly answered by Samuel Zenas Ammen, who utilized the same arguments over and over in rebuttal. Ammen's efforts were so successful that he, in 1916, could observe:

> I opposed Northern extension to devote the fraternity to a Southern purpose. But for me, Northern extension would have happened decades ago. In many articles in the *Journal* and in KA history, I have, while fighting Northern extension, insisted that our purpose was to conserve Southern Ideals.[37]

It would be, no doubt, too simplistic to agree with Ammen that he alone kept the fraternity primarily in the South. Yet, it can be truly said that his efforts in this regard far excelled the efforts of any other fraternity member. To combat Northern extension, Ammen intensified the Southern rhetoric of the organization in his contributions to the *Journal* and in his articles on fraternity history which appeared in the fraternity catalogues. He, as author of the ritual, had originally drafted the aims and purposes of the organization. Ammen therefore occupied a unique position as the undisputed interpreter of his own sacred text, a position which others were not wont to regard lightly. Thus, while Knight Commander from 1891 to 1897, and for many years afterward, Ammen continued to mold the organization to fit his own notions of Southern sectionalism. And although he publicly disclaimed sectional considerations regarding the fraternity, his private utterances indicate that the opposite was the case. In a letter concerning ritual revision, written to former Knight Commander Dan Neal in 1891, Ammen wrote:

> Particularly would I wish the degrees and changes to smack all of "Dixie," to find examples of great character and achievement in Southern annals.... I should favor making the existing degrees so Dixieish as to diminish the probability of any yankee being initiated or the Order taken North.[38]

Yet, in spite of his authoritative position, Ammen could not have successfully prevented Northern extension, nor could he have wrapped the organization in the garment of the Southern mystique without the consent of the general membership. The dearth in numbers among those who favored Northern extension would seem to indicate that he had that consent. Because of Ammen's strong sectional bias, and because of the sentiments of a large majority of the membership, Kappa Alpha restricted its activity to the far West, to the border states, and above all, to the South, where its strength continued to lie at least well into the last part of the twentieth century. But sensitive to outside criticism, the leaders of the fraternity steadfastly maintained that their decision to remain in the South arose from reasons other than sectional considerations:

> For better or for worse, our lot has been irreclaimably cast on the south. There we are destined to work out the problems of brotherhood in our own particular way. It may not be the best way, but it will be our own, and though our policy may be decried as sectional by those unable to appreciate our motives, it is a comfort to reflect that there are things more to be deplored which come from a campaign of chapter-building by the wholesale.[39]

Yet, it can only be concluded that these disclaimed sectional considerations embodied the very reasons why the KAs repeatedly refused to enter the Northern states. Although much has been written on the subject, the impact of Confederate defeat upon the white people of the South can never be overly stressed. Ammen, and the majority of the KA leaders, became engulfed in the wave of Southern bitterness which spread like a typhoon through the Southern states in the years following the Civil War. It was a bitterness which at a gut level conceded a good bit of hate toward outsiders, especially the North, but a bitterness which on a superficial level capitulated to the rhetoric of reconciliation of the time. Thus, while disclaiming sectionalism and hatred of Yankees, the KAs stayed out of the North and arduously sought to preserve Southern values precisely for those reasons. Southern bitterness worked to prevent Northern extension.

Chapter V

✣   ✣   ✣

THE LOST CAUSE, SOUTHERN HISTORY, AND ROBERT E. LEE

Widespread "Confederate-ization" of the fraternity did not come until the early years of the twentieth century, when Robert E. Lee was officially canonized as the "patron saint" of the organization. Still, earlier generations of KAs definitely subscribed to Romantic notions of the Old South and the Confederacy, notions which worked themselves into the fabric of the organization and became vital to it. For in a very real sense, conceding that the stated purpose of the organization was "the cultivation of virtues and graces conceived to be distinctively Southern," the presuppositions upon which this purpose was based involved a definite interpretation of Southern history and the Southern experience.[1] And, thus, it is to the KAs' understanding of their collective experience as Southerners that we now direct our attention.

In addition to the writings of Samuel Zenas Ammen, articles concerning the South and the Confederacy appeared in the *Kappa Alpha Journal* between the years of 1879 and 1898. These articles assumably mirrored the attitudes of the readers of the *Journal*, as well as those of their authors. While never profuse, they appeared with increased regularity between 1885 and 1889, roughly during the editorships of Horace Henry White and Walter W. Brown. In the 1880s, the early period of the magazine's existence when fraternity journalism was still in its infancy and the role of the *Kappa Alpha Journal* was not yet clearly defined, articles of an historical, political, and literary nature frequently appeared within its pages. However, by the 1890s, the *Journal* dealt almost entirely with fraternity topics and such articles decreased in number. In later decades, occasional articles appeared in the *Journal* that expressed Southern attitudes toward Southern history. However, issues of the magazine prior to 1890, especially during the late 1880s, provide the broadest sample of KA attitudes toward the South. From these earlier issues of the *Journal* a pattern of how KA writers viewed Southern history can be reconstructed.

Like many Southern writers of the postbellum period, the authors whose works appeared in the *Kappa Alpha Journal* seemed to be writing as if they were standing upon the ash heap of a destroyed civilization. And in their writings that civilization, the Old South, became transformed by means of sentimental nostalgia into sort of a Golden Age. They sheared it of brutal actuality and embellished it into a folk mythology that stood in juxtaposition to the poverty, defeat, and ruthless materialism of the postbellum era as a time of beauty, grace, and culture, and, above all, a time of chivalry:

True it is, and true to nature, that the Southerner often sighs his soul away to the chivalric days before the war, and they are to him the "good old days." The old mansion, surrounded by royal landscape, dotted with statuary, arbors, walks leading to rambling conservatories wherein the canary and mocking bird piped their tuneful lays from orange bough or wreath of rose; the slave to wait at every call, the blooded horse, the swift footed hound — all are gone. Those were times such as the South will never see again; a summer day, when hospitality, chivalry, grace, courage, devotion, beauty, wit, and culture reign enchanted all with a happy remembrance....[2]

Chivalry ruled supreme, enshrined in the society of the Old South; and the Southern planter, the prototypical old Southern gentleman, through the refinement engendered by classical education and through the paternalistic feeling inspired through the care of his slaves, rose to a status of high individual character unpolluted by a crass desire for materialistic gain.[3]

But ultimately this beautiful world of grace and honor came to be destroyed by a brutal war, an unavoidable war with the materialistic North. The War came as a difference of opinion between the two sections in regard to the limitations of the federal government. It arose as a contest between the ideas of centralization and states rights.[4] When the South seceded, it vindicated the Constitution, which had guaranteed the right of secession.[5] But also, the Civil War came as an attempt by unprincipled Northern men, spurred on by ambition and greed, to subjugate and bring havoc upon the South:

> We of the South know that this fiendish lust for power and fame has wrapped us in its blighting folds; has slain our noblest manhood in a fraternal war; has dared to attack the sacred constitution of our country — the proudest heritage of Southern blood and brain, . . . *low ambition* lit the first fires of fanatic hate and led armies invaders of defenseless homes. . . .[6]

Then, ultimately, the War came as a clash between two conflicting civilizations — one, the South, the repository of chivalry and spiritual values, and the other, the North, the stronghold of materialistic greed.

But the South did not readily capitulate to invading Yankee armies. For,

> . . . proud we may be to know that this crusade of unholy gain and glory which swept over our land, was met by men who could forget their own brief lives, and dared to die for the cause of their country and the honor of their homes.[7]

Southern chivalry rallied and fought nobly in defense of the Southern homeland. "The Spirit of Chivalry" has found no higher exemplification than was witnessed in the heroic struggles of the

Southern Confederacy to maintain its position as a nation, among the nations of the earth.[8]

But although the heroic and chivalric sons of the South fought hard and bravely and many of them gave their lives for the cause, the South, although armed with the right, lost the war. And this one fact, the reality of defeat, was the most difficult of all for the KA writers, as well as for many Southerners to comprehend. For if the Confederacy represented all that was right, good, and noble, how could it be that the experiment in Southern nationalism came to be only an exercise in futility? How could it be that so many thousands of Southern lives were given up in vain? How could it be that victory eventually came to a cheating, mercenary Northern society? For if the society of the Old South and the Confederacy rested upon eternal values, it was impossible to think that these societies could be swept away. Thus, Southerners, including the KAs, in their quandary came to the opinion that although old Southern society had been erased, the values upon which that society was based, the values of chivalry, being eternal, could never be erased. Consequently, somehow, in a mystic fashion that was possible in an age grounded in idealistic philosophy, out of defeat came victory, and out of Southern devastation came the apotheosis of the Lost Cause. Out of Confederate defeat came the Confederate Myth.

The Confederacy, in actuality, was riddled with poor government, widespread desertion in its armies, continual threats of rebellion within its borders, lack of co-operation from state governors, and wholesale corruption. Nonetheless, through the efforts of postbellum writers and orators, it became in defeat the supreme period of Southern unity, heroism, and devotion. The Cause, while it never received complete support in the South during its real existence, came to have unified support after its defeat. Its values, which to the KAs were the values of chivalry, rose triumphant, victorious in defeat:

> Out of the depths of her [the South's] despair, the Old South, the unconquerable spirit of the Old South arose beatified and triumphant.... It was the immortal Spirit of Chivalry, the quenchless flame, that burned like an altar fire amid all disasters.[9]

In essence, mind had prevailed over matter, the spiritual over the material, if not in actuality, then in the minds of the faithful. And thus, the KAs saw themselves as the preservers of the Cause Triumphant, the eternal spirit of chivalry, the overriding, enduring Idea of the Old South and the defeated Confederacy:

> It is, in truth, to the society of the Old Dominion and of the Old South that we look for the fullest realization of our ideals, and

while others lay claim to the honor, it cannot be doubted that the Kappa Alpha fraternity is the chosen repository of those eternal verities, and to her, more than to any other organization established during the war, they have been entrusted to preserve and inculcate among her members, We may humbly hope to approach but we can never surpass the high type of chivalrous manhood which the society of the Old South produced, and, as breathing the true "Spirit of Chivalry," and setting forth the models of manhood which we most desire to imitate.[10]

Yet, although they paid regular tribute to the cult of the Lost Cause, at times the KA writers of the late 1880s exhibited a willingness to accept the verdict of the war and to work for a complete reconciliation of the sections. All agreed that the questions of secession and slavery had been totally settled by the war, and that the South would faithfully abide by the decision of the conflict:

> . . . Southern honor which is far dearer than Southern blood, stands pledged that this decision shall be a final settlement of the questions at issue. And cursed be he who born on Southern soil and inheriting the traditional honor and chivalry of Southern manhood, shall tarnish his own fair name and disgrace a noble ancestry by raising his voice to reverse that decision.[11]

One writer went so far as to suggest that the South might have been wrong in the War, although he agreed with the others in proclaiming that the South had acted rightly in fighting the North. In effect, he stated that the South had been right and wrong at the same time:

> Let us dwell for a moment on another topic—the feeling the South cherishes toward the North and toward the Union. In the first place, I say that the South has nothing to take back — nothing for which to apologize. She did her duty, or what she deemed to be her duty, and I do not hesitate to say that had I a predecessor who lived in the South at the time of the war and did not follow the example of Lee and Jackson, I would be ashamed of him today. But the God who holds the balance of power in his hand gave the victory to the North. We know why now. Slavery was a curse in the sight of God, and the Union must conquer or perish. A wiser Leader than any we know decided, and for the best. With the light the South had to guide her I am glad she acted as she did and glad she was whipped. I am glad that slavery, feudalism, and serfdom are banished from our glorious country forever. . . . The South has ceased to worry about sectional hatred and animosity. She loves the Union.[12]

Thus, the writers in the *Kappa Alpha Journal* in the late 1880s demonstrated a willingness for reconciliation combined with a great pride in their Confederate past. They expressed a conviction that although their Confederate fathers had lost the war, they had at least fought nobly and bravely, and that cursed be those who dared question their motives for fighting were anything other than honorable and true. The desire for reconciliation with the North, while often sincere, was yet more often mitigated with a great deal of bitterness, the bitterness of a proud people who had been forced to endure defeat and poverty.

But out of the defeat and poverty of the Reconstruction years came a vision of a South restored to its former position of economic prominence. This vision of a New South, was proclaimed by Henry Grady, the editor of the Atlanta *Constitution*, as a doctrine which urged industrial development and the investment of Northern capital into Southern enterprises. This doctrine, known to historians as the New South Creed, evoked, as C. Van Woodward has pointed out in his *Origins of the New South*, a divided response among Southerners. Likewise, it evoked a divided response among the KA authors under discussion. Some of them eagerly welcomed the idea of Southern industrial development:

> After four years of war, and twelve of misrule, in 1876, one-hundred years after the declaration of independence, the South renewed that sainted compact, and Sphinx-like, rising from her ashes, placed herself once more on the high road to that prosperity which she had known so well in ante bellum days. When the smoke of her furnaces shall herald the rising sun and the music of her anvils beat tatoo [sic] of his setting, then, I have thought, will the throne of commercial empire, deserting the precincts of Boston, Lowell, and Pittsburgh, find its destined resting place on the banks of the Savannah, the Alabama, and the Mississippi.[13]

On the other hand, others saw only the threat of Yankee materialism in the prospect of industrialization, and they refused to make a distinction between the New South and the Old:

> We believe that the South is the descendant of the ante bellum South, and that the development of the present is but expansion of the germs. Why is there so much prodigal-son-returned-talk about the New South. The South of today is the South of our fathers. We may admit our father's mistakes, but we should never, by implication, impugn their wisdom, worth, and integrity by admitting a difference between the "Old" and "New South."

> Southern newspapers act like Northern wealth and Northern immigration is the *sine qua non* without which our land is ever to remain in of despondency. With beggerly [sic] importunity they do sue for the investment of Northern wealth and the inrush of Northern people. Money is needed to produce the quickest and greatest material improvement, but would this material blessing overbalance the evil results which arise from the inroad of an overwhelming number of Northern laborers, with their low grade of social life and socialistic tendencies? What benefit is there for us

to be turned from an agricultural to a manufacturing people? Should the "Solid South" discard its pride, independence, chivalry, and for arguments sake, POVERTY, for the loose materialism and groveling ideas of a bartering, trading, cheating commercial people? Should Esau sell his birthright for a mess of pottage?[14]

Probably this condemnation of Southern attempts to woo Northern industry and Northern profit more nearly expressed the official rhetoric of Kappa Alpha. For most of the articles which appeared in the *Kappa Alpha Journal* during these years seem to have had in common a tendency to polarize the North and South as material versus spiritual, and as mercenary versus chivalric, a polarization which partly has its roots in the ritual of the fraternity, and which also was suggested in the later writings of Samuel Zenas Ammen:

> Kappa Alpha's mission in the academic world is to withstand sordid materialistic tendencies, by insisting upon the value of the spiritual aspirations and lofty ideals which are our people's best inheritance. Wealth is to be sought as means to the end of comfort, education, and broad culture, but regard must be had, above all, for the intangibles, the possession of which dignifies life, and gives it real value. This quest is our perennial mission.[15]

Thus, if the fraternity existed to preserve the spiritual and chivalric values of the Old South, it would naturally have to stand in judgment of the "materialism" of the North and the "materialistic tendencies" of the "New" South.

Widely influenced by the all pervasive romanticism of the period and the "great man theory" of history, and writing before the advent of critical, scholarly history, the anonymous KA writers in question generally interpreted Southern history as glorious and heroic. For them that history had a didactic purpose. They saw it as a chronicle of the noble deeds of great men, recorded to inspire Southern youth to greatness:

> The Southern youth who has the heritage his father left him in a life consecrated to the service of his country [the Confederacy] in maintaining his convictions, is the possessor of what riches could never give him — a heritage that should inspire him until he overcame difficulty and danger, until he conquered even death itself.[16]

Thus, imbued with a sense of hero worship for the leaders of the Southern past, it was only natural that the KAs should eventually appropriate a hero for their very own, a hero from Southern history who would symbolize the heroic and chivalric virtues which they held in such high esteem.

The story of how Robert E. Lee came to be revered as the "Spiritual Founder" of the Kappa Alpha fraternity, was largely a phenomenon of the twentieth century. It therefore logically lies outside the bounds of this study, which has heretofore devoted itself to nineteenth-century developments. But in that the movement to single out Lee for veneration represents the culmination of the process through which the fraternity chose to wrap itself in the mantle of the Southern tradition and the Southern mystique, it will be considered here.

As previously indicated, it is doubtful that General Lee had any part in the founding of Kappa Alpha at Washington College while he was president of that institution from 1865 to 1870. Still, as alluded to earlier, a legend to that effect grew up in fraternity circles during the latter years of the nineteenth century. The first reference to Lee's possible connection to KA did not appear in a printed fraternity source until 1887. Then, an article in the *Kappa Alpha Journal* stated:

> There are several floating rumors and beautiful stories about the origin of KA at Washington and Lee University. One of these stories which has become very widespread and one which would certainly make our Order more beloved and cherished even than it now is, if firmly established as a matter of fact, is to the effect that General Robert Lee took quite an important part in the organization of KA.[17]

Although none of the founders of the fraternity appeared to have immediately confirmed the rumor, the legend obviously continued. It was not mentioned again in print until 1897, when Samuel Zenas Ammen, who was in a position to know the validity of the story, referred to it in the first KA rush manual, *Kappa Alpha in '97*:

> There is a persistent, but unverifiable tradition in the fraternity that General Lee took a special interest in the young organization and influenced the formation of its character...."[18]

Thus, while not confirming nor denying the story, Ammen allowed it to continue.

The real impetus to the movement to adopt Lee as the exemplar of the fraternity came in 1901. Robert Edward Pritchard, editor of the *Kappa Alpha Journal*, in an article in the January issue of that year, called the whole fraternity to adopt Lee as the "patron saint" of the Order and to celebrate his birthday, 19 January, with annual banquets:

> It was during Lee's presidency of Washington College that Kappa Alpha Order was founded. It has been handed down to us as a beautiful tradition that this great man took a peculiar interest in K. A. We do not claim him as our founder, nor even as a member, though we wish we could do so, but we do claim him to be our ideal of the man. And it is to the reaching of this ideal that all the

General Robert E. Lee

*Print Published by C. Bohn
Richmond, Virginia
Private Collection*

teachings of our Order tend, You cannot take a better example for your life than that of the man of whom not the slightest word of reproach can be truthfully spoken... Let every member of our Order then honor his birthday. Every chapter alumni and active, should celebrate it — and the more you emulate him, the more fit and ready will you be when the Day of Judgment comes. Well may he be our patron Saint. Well may he be our example of the man in whose mold we wish to be cast. There is one country now, true enough; yet there is one Robert Edward Lee, and he is the hero of Southern and Kappa Alpha hearts.[19]

Pritchard's idea seems to have been adopted immediately, for very soon afterward subsequent issues of the *Journal* began to refer to Lee as the "patron saint" of the fraternity and to record news of KA banquets at which tributes to Lee were spoken.[20]

The semi-centennial convention of the fraternity, held at Richmond, Virginia in December 1915, brought further identification of Lee with Kappa Alpha. Three early members of Alpha Chapter, Dr. William Nelson Scott, Dr. Stanhope McClelland Scott, and Col. Jo Lane Stern, appeared at the convention and testified to the influence that General Lee had over the Kappa Alpha students at Washington College. Moreover, before the convention adjourned, the delegates solemnly gathered at the base of the Lee monument in Richmond, where they silently placed a wreath.[21]

In 1921, Thomas Dixon, Jr., popular Southern novelist and a member of the fraternity, dedicated his fictionalized biography of Lee, *The Man in Grey*, to the members of the Kappa Alpha Order. In the dedication he proclaimed the fraternity was "founded under the influence of Robert Edward Lee."[22] But the final link connecting Lee with KA was forged at the 1923 convention in Washington, D.C. There former Knight Commander and noted Southern orator, John Temple Graves, in a highly romanticized banquet toast, dubbed Lee as the "Spiritual Founder of the Order:"

> Robert E. Lee inspired and visualized in actual living the matchless Ritual of our fraternity, and his name will live in our hearts and in human history forever. Ammen was the practical Founder, and for more than half a century has held the heart of Kappa Alpha; Lee was the spiritual Founder. The real toast to the real Founder has never yet been written or spoken. Let us speak it here tonight. It will not pluck one leaf from the laurels of Ammen. There is neither need nor room for another star in the diaden [sic] which history has fashioned for Lee. But the spirit of Lee inspired the spirit of Ammen; the fingers of Lee had touched the fingers of Ammen who wrote the Creed.
>
> Knights, Gentlemen, Brethren:
> Lift high your glasses here tonight, and in the liquid spotless as his fame let us pledge for all time the Spiritual Founder — the first,

last, and incomparable Knight Commander of the Kappa Alpha Order — Robert Edward Lee of old Virginia!²³

Samuel Zenas Ammen, who was in his eighties in 1923, was deeply hurt by Graves' eulogizing. Ammen had privately opposed the Scott brothers' attempts in 1915 at giving Lee credit as the inspiration for the fraternity. In a revealing letter in 1924, dated several months after Graves had made the toast to Lee as "Spiritual Founder," Ammen wrote:

> There is one story which tradition or legend building is constructing which does me injustice, being absolutely unfounded: namely that Gen. Lee is the author of our ritual, — "guided my hand," in writing it, according to J. Temple Graves in the January *Journal*.
>
> General Lee has glory enough without giving him what little may accrue to me, from having one bright idea when a boy. You no doubt know all about it. Gen. Lee probably never heard of K. A. He never had a word with any K. A about it. He never talked to me about it, or suggested anything. He was not partial to K. A.'s.
>
> He dismissed Wood from college Feb, 1, 1867 because Wood was learning nothing. He was near preventing me from continuing at college in Sept. 1867 by insisting when I asked him that he could not let me get credit for my tuition for my Second session, Took no interest in it, — Tho' in my first session (66-67), I had won distinguished on every subject, — I had studied. My father died in June '67, and no cash was then available. The catalogue said such as I could get credit on tuition, but Gen. Lee did not know that, — and evidently did not care a dam [*sic*].
>
> I reminded him of the catalogue statement. *Then*, he agreed, without pleasure to put my name on a list for the faculty to consider. So he was not admired by me. Had I not returned in '67, there would have been no K. A. Did Lee found us?²⁴

Ammen was perhaps overzealous about guarding his position of principal founder and creator of the fraternity, especially as he had promoted the Lee connection a time or two himself. The fact remains that his letters were generally frank, to the point, and reliable. Still, at the time of Graves' speech, Ammen was getting to be a very old man, and he was genuinely grieved in his belief that his position of honor was being usurped by banquet speech rhetoric. In spite of Ammen's private protestations, Graves' toast came to be adopted as the official toast for all KA banquets held on 19 January, Lee's birthday.²⁵ Thus, Robert E. Lee came to be the "Spiritual Founder" of the Fraternity, giving the KAs an historical embodiment of chivalric ideals. The fact that Lee, according to Ammen, had originally had nothing to do with KA made little difference, as reality faded into foggy mythology, through the grand eloquent oratory of after dinner speechmakers.

The Conquered Banner

*From
Father Ryan's Poems
New York
1903*

And, consequently, with all of its baggage of Southern attitudes, Southern heroes, and Southern tradition firmly attached, Kappa Alpha as a mythic vehicle could make its way slowly through the twentieth century, carrying with it the entire mystique of "Southernism." Although in later years, Old South costume balls, secession speeches, rebel flags, Confederate uniforms, and replicas of Civil War cannon would be added, the mold of the organization had been cast many years earlier. It began largely through the efforts of Samuel Zenas Ammen, but in the end, in spite of Samuel Zenas Ammen.

Chapter VI

✛   ✛   ✛

THE MIND OF THE NEW SOUTH

Kappa Alpha Order was born in reaction. Its founders and early formulators, notably Samuel Zenas Ammen, conceived the organization to be, first and foremost, a vehicle to preserve selected attitudes of white Southern culture, which, because of the reverses caused by the Civil War, seemed to be threatened with extinction. Thus, it arose not only as a college fraternity, but also as one of several post-war Southern organizations dedicated to the task of preserving Southern values and glorifying the Southern past. Others in this constellation include the Southern Historical Society, the United Confederate Veterans, and the United Daughters of the Confederacy. In a real sense, the KAs acted as sort of collegiate wing of the UDC. This became increasingly true into the twentieth century, as the fraternity began to change into more of a social organization which adopted the use of Confederate flags, Old South costume parties, secession ceremonies, and the veneration of Robert E. Lee.

As a result, Kappa Alpha never has been "just another college fraternity." Heavily influenced by the Southern ideals of its founders, most notably Ammen, and by the conditions of its founding in the Valley of Virginia shortly after the Civil War, the fraternity has been committed to the preservation of almost the entire mythic structure of the "Southern tradition." But to its credit, although KA has numbered among its membership some of the more prominent apostles of Southern racism, never in its history did the organization itself overtly stoop to promote racist feeling, except for the fact that it once excluded Negroes from membership. During most of its history it existed in a totally non-reflective racist society, the segregated South. And although the fraternity as an organization never officially espoused racist rhetoric, in another sense, it stood as a support to Southern racist society, in that it aided in fostering a vision of the Southern past as pristine and as a heroic and glorious drama. The fraternity taught through its ritual and through its Confederate trappings that the Golden Age, the paradigm, existed in the past: in the Old South, in the Confederacy, and during the Age of Chivalry, and that while these societies themselves have been lost, the values upon which they rested must be preserved.

Yet, if Kappa Alpha glorified the Southern past and affirmed the "Southern way of life," so did almost the entire postbellum Southern white population. The KAs, however, were not merely reflective of a society intent upon ancestor worship and envisioning Romantic air castles in which the graces of chivalry, honor, and beauty did dwell. The establishment of the fraternity as a preserver of the clustered myths of "Southernism" came not by accident. Rather, it was cast in its mold by design, the design of Ammen and other creators of the organization. Thus, instead of being a mere reflection of the folk notions of white Southern society, Kappa Alpha took an active role in promoting and perpetuating such notions. This was a small role perhaps and was largely restricted to fraternity membership. But nonetheless, it was a significant role, especially as its members assumed political and other leadership positions in the mid-twentieth century

In the postbellum decades Kappa Alpha aided in the process through which a defeated and confounded people found meaning and nobility in their tragic history. By existing as one of many organizations which glorified the Southern past and affirmed the "Southern way of life," Kappa Alpha also contributed to that peculiar affinity of white Southerners to shut out criticism and questioning of their "way of life."

By the mid-twentieth century, serious attacks were made on the fortress of "Southern tradition." In recent decades Southern historians have turned from descriptions of Confederate Cavaliers to a critical evaluation of the Southern past, bringing into focus perspectives of the slave, freed blacks, and poor whites, as well. As a result, the *Gone With The Wind* interpretation of Southern history has fallen into disrepute. The Civil Rights Movement has done much to call into judgment traditional Southern notions of caste and class. The women's rights movement questioned a passive, if protected role for women. Casual lifestyles have eroded old courtly manners. Abrasive elbowing and rude behavior have replaced deferential courtesy.

With such attacks on its tradition, symbols, and world view Kappa Alpha remains as a repository of the aspirations and values of a former age. It is now fully integrated, racially and ethnically. Whether it will continue to uphold its genteel tradition depends on the tolerance and pluralism of our society, its willingness to surrender cheerfully any residual racism, and the dedication of its members. Kappa Alpha's emphasis on thoughtful kindness, devotion to women, honor, noble idealism, and personal achievemnt may be eternal verities which will see it through the sea of change. There yet may be something for future generations to learn, not from the faults, but from the highest values of the old Southern ruling culture -- of which Robert E. Lee was the finest expression.

Engraving From
The Knights Templars by C. G. Addison
New York
1874

APPENDIX A

APPENDIX

CHAPTER LIST. 1865-1899

Name	Location		Date of Establishment
1 Alpha	Washington and Lee University	Lexington, Virginia	Dec. 21, 1865
2 Beta	Virginia Military Institute	Lexington, Virginia	March 8, 1868
3 Gamma	University of Georgia	Athens, Georgia	April 6, 1868
4 Delta	Wofford College	Spartanburg, S.C.	Feb. 23, 1869
5 Epsilon	Emory College	Oxford, Georgia	June 4, 1869
6 Zeta	Randolph Macon College	Ashland, Virginia	Nov. 26, 1869
7 Eta	Richmond College	Richmond, Virginia	Mar. 18, 1870
8 Theta (prime)	Oglethorpe University	Atlanta, Georgia (1872)	Dec. 25, 1870
9 Iota	Furman University	Greenville. S.C. (1898)	May 8, 1872
10 Kappa	Mercer University	Macon, Georgia	Nov. 8, 1873
11 Lambda	University of Virginia	Charlottesville, Va.	Nov. 18, 1873
12 Mu (prime)	Newberry College	Walhalla, S.C. (1876)	Nov. 26, 1873
13 Omicron (prime)	Bethel Academy	Fauquier County, Va.	Oct. —, 1878
14 Pi (prime)	Gordon Institute	Barnesville, Georgia	April 18, 1879
15 Sigma	Davidson College	Davidson, N.C.	Feb. 18, 1880
16 Rho	South Carolina College	Columbia, S.C. (1897)	Jan. 4, 1881
17 Tau	Wake Forest College	Wake Forest, N.C. (1894)	Jan. 8, 1881
18 Upsillon	University of North Carolina	Chapel Hill, N.C.	Nov. 25, 1881
19 Psi	Tulane University	New Orleans, La.	Jan. 14, 1882
20 Phi	Southern University	Greensboro, Alabama	Jan. 17, 1882
21 Chi	Vanderbilt University	Nashville, Tennessee	April 9, 1883
22 Omega	Centre College	Danville, Kentucky	Sept. 4, 1883
23 Theta (second)	S. C. Military Academy	Charleston, S.C. (1890)	Oct. 1, 1883
24 Omicron	University of Texas	Austin, Texas	Oct. 5, 1883
25 Mu (second)	Erskine College	Due West, S.C. (1893)	Nov. 14, 1883
26 Nu	Alabama A. & M. College	Auburn, Alabama	Nov. 24, 1883
27 Xi	Southwestern University	Georgetown, Texas	Nov. 28, 1883
28 Pi	University of Tennessee	Knoxville, Tennessee	Dec. 1, 1883
29 A-Alpha	University of the South	Sewanee, Tennessee	Dec. 1, 1883
30 A-Beta	University of Alabama	Tuscaloosa, Alabama	June 17, 1885
31 A-Gamma	Louisiana State University	Baton Rouge, La.	July 2, 1885
32 A-Delta	William Jewell College	Liberty, Missouri	Feb. 5, 1887
33 A-Epsilon	S. W. Presbyterian University	Clarksville, Tennessee	Nov. 16, 1887
34 A-Zeta	William and Mary College	Williamsburg, Virginia	Jan. 3, 1890
35 A-Eta	Westminster College	Fulton, Missouri	Feb. 5, 1890
36 A-Theta	Kentucky University	Lexington, Kentucky	Apr. 9, 1891
37 A-Iota	Centenary College	Jackson, Louisiana	Sept. 14, 1891
38 A-Kappa	Missouri State University	Columbia, Missouri	Sept. 30, 1891
39 A-Lambda	Johns Hopkins University	Baltimore, Maryland.	Oct. 21, 1891
40 Theta	Kentucky State College	Lexington, Kentucky	Feb. 21, 1893
41 A-Mu	Millsaps College	Jackson, Mississippi	Oct. 1, 1893
42 Mu (third)	Emory & Henry College	Emory, Virignia (1895)	Dec. 21, 1893
43 A-Nu	Columbian University	Washington, D.C.	Nov. 18, 1894
44 A-Xi	University of California	Berkeley, California	Mar. 6, 1894

Chapter List (Cont'd)

Name	Location		Date of Establishment
45 A-Omicron	University of Arkansas	Fayetteville, Arkansas	Apr. 27, 1895
46 A-Pi	Leland Stanford, Jr., University	Palo Alto, Calif.	Oct. 27, 1895
47 A-Rho	West Virginia University	Morgantown, W. Va.	March 10, 897
48 A-Sigma	Georgia School of Technology	Atlanta, Georgia	Oct. 21, 1899
49 A-Tau	Hampden Sidney College	Hampden Sidney, Va.	Dec. 6, 1899
50 A-Upsilon	University of Mississippi	Oxford, Mississippi	Jan. 12, 1900

The order of the alphabet has been followed in the naming of the chapters, with the following exceptions: The names Nu and Xi (prime) were set apart for chapters that failed to be established. For no apparent reason Sigma was established before Rho and Psi before Phi and Chi. When a chapter was dead beyond hope of revival its name was given to another.

APPENDIX B

FOUNDING DATE OF KAPPA ALPHA

A long and embroiled controversy over the founding date of Kappa Alpha has never been resolved. Traditionally the date of founding has been 21 December 1865. Although this date has been used in all fraternity publications since 1893, it has been questioned many times. During the 1870s and 1880s, the 21 December date passed down through the chapters as a tradition and it was generally accepted. Still, it could not be confirmed, because the minutes of Alpha Chapter had been lost.

In 1893, Tazewell Taylor Hubard, Grand Historian of the fraternity asked Samuel Zenas Ammen, who was then Knight Commander, to help him settle on an exact founding date that could to be used in the historical records and publications of the fraternity. Hubard and Ammen decided to accept the traditional date of 21 December 1865, and printed the notice of their decision in the February 1893 issue of the *Kappa Alpha Journal* without comment. Ammen and Hubard based their decision upon the fraternity tradition of long standing, and Ammen used the curious method of translating the letters K. A. into their symbolic numerical equivalents, K-20, A-1, and added them together to get 21. Thus, he reasoned, if KA symbolically means 21, the founding date must have been on the twenty-first of December.

Very soon after this decision was made, the Alpha Chapter minutes were found again in someone's attic. After reading the minutes Hubard and Ammen became skeptical about the date they had chosen, because while the minutes for the 1865-1866 school year were missing, the minutes of November 1867, referred to the "Anniversary Celebration" on April 9. The recovered minutes went on to show that on 13 December 1867, the members of Alpha Chapter changed the "Anniversary Celebration" from 9 April to 21 December, and from thenceforth the "Anniversary Celebration" was held yearly during the last week of December. Could it be that the fraternity was founded on 9 April 1866 instead of 21 December 1865? Ammen and Hubard were not sure. Others pointed out that "Anniversary Celebration" did not necessarily mean the anniversary of the founding; rather, it could have easily meant the anniversary of Lee's surrender. So, Hubard and Ammen let the matter drop, and the date of 21 December 1865 continued to be carried in fraternity publications. Also, the December date seemed to be confirmed by William Nelson Scott, who in 1898, in a letter to Ammen and in an article in the May 1898 issue of the *Kappa Alpha Journal*, stated that the fraternity was formed in December of 1865.

In 1900, the fraternity received from the family of William A. Walsh, who was one of the four founders, a printed receipt. It was for a $1.00 initiation fee made out to William A. Walsh and signed by James Ward Wood. The receipt was dated "May 9, 1866." This raised another question. If Walsh was one of the original founders, and if the fraternity was founded on 21 December 1865, why did Walsh, who was a financially solvent young man, pay his initiation fee so late? Consequently, Ammen began to question the 21 December date.

On 16 June 1915, Reverend William Nelson Scott visited Ammen and at that time, Ammen pointed out to Scott that the Alpha Minutes suggested 9 April as the founding date. To this Scott replied that even if the minutes suggest organization on 9 April, there must have been a period of discussion and preparation for the founding before the end of 1865. Thus, Scott wavered on December 1865 as being the absolute date of founding and favored a gradual period of evolution, covering several months. Scott did not live very long after his visit with Ammen. Consequently, this was his final word on the subject.

Hoping to settle the matter once and for all, Leroy Stafford Boyd, a KA interested in fraternity history, visited James Ward Wood at Wood's home in West Virginia in 1918. Wood, true to form, was very vague and metaphoric, but he did tell Boyd that KA was founded as Phi Kappa Chi shortly before Christmas 1865. Wood also stated that 9 April was probably celebrated as the "Anniversary" of Lee's surrender.

Then, something very strange happened. Ammen wrote Stanhope McClelland Scott, the fourth original founder, and asked Scott his opinion on when the fraternity was founded. Scott replied that he would look into the matter. The result was that Stanhope Scott showed up at the KA National Convention in Washington with two affidavits, one signed by himself and one signed by James Ward Wood. Both affidavits stated that Kappa Alpha met for the first time on 9 April 1866, the anniversary of Lee's surrender. Scott then asked the convention to settle the matter by voting to accept 9 April 1866 as the official founding date of the fraternity, to which the convention agreed by unanimous vote. This decision was quickly buried in the convention minutes, because fraternity publications continued to carry the 21 December 1865 date. Shortly after the 1923 convention, Samuel Zenas Ammen wrote an article for the KA *Journal* affirming the April 1866 date, but the article was courteously returned to Ammen by the editor. In 1927, Leroy S. Boyd wrote an article for the *Kappa Alpha Journal,* which was printed. He argued for the December 1865 date. This seems to have ended the matter, because in spite of the decision of the 1923 convention, fraternity national officers were unwilling to change the traditional founding date. Nonetheless, both Stanhope McClelland Scott and Samuel Zenas Ammen maintained to their deaths that the fraternity was founded on 9 April 1866.

Before drawing my conclusions, I considered the conflicting reports, plus the following pertinent facts. In a letter to G. D. Letcher, Stanhope Scott mentions a toast in his possession in James Ward Wood's handwriting. It was to "the two Williams," and was dated "December 21, 1865." Scott said in the letter that the "two Williams" were William Nelson Scott, his brother, and William A. Walsh, and that the toast was given in Walsh's room. This proves that Wood, Nelson Scott, and Walsh were meeting together in Walsh's room as early as December 1865. Therefore, I believe that, as Wood stated to Boyd, the three of them formed Phi Kappa Chi in late December 1865. Further, I believe that the fraternity evolved gradually over a period of months; that Stanhope Scott joined the original three shortly after he entered college in January 1866; that sometime in the early spring of 1866, Harry Estill of Phi Kappa Psi asked Wood to change the name of the new group; and that the fraternity was re-established as Kappa Alpha Fraternity on 9 April 1866.

Thus, according to this interpretation, the "Anniversary Celebration" of the Alpha Chapter minutes commemorated the refounding of the fraternity as Kappa Alpha, and Walsh thus received one month later the receipt for his initiation into the newly reformed fraternity. Perhaps the founders, when they changed the name, wanted to make a new beginning, a fresh start, because Phi Kappa Chi proved to be an embarrassment to them, since it was so obviously an attempt to copy Phi Kappa Psi.

NOTES

Preface

1 George Brown Tindall, "Southern Mythology," *The Idea of the South*, ed. Frank Everson Vandiver (Chicago: Published for William Marsh Rice University by the University of Chicago Press, 1964), 2.

2 Ibid., 8-10.

Chapter I
THE FOUNDING

1 Samuel Zenas Ammen, "Wood as Founder," Unpublished manuscript, Samuel Zenas Ammen Collection, National Administrative Office, Kappa Alpha Order, Atlanta (Hereinafter cited as Ammen Collection.).

2 Dr. Olinger Crenshaw, Chairman of the Department of History, Washington and Lee University, interview by author, Lexington, Virginia, 16 April 1967.

3 Samuel Zenas Ammen, "Judge James Ward Wood," *Kappa Alpha Journal* XV (May 1898), 336 (Hereinafter cited as Ammen, "Judge James Ward Wood.").

4 Samuel Zenas Ammen, "James Ward Wood, A Sketch," First Copy Book, Ammen Collection, 51 (Hereinafter cited as Ammen, "James Ward Wood, A Sketch".).

5 Samuel Zenas Ammen, "Wood as Founder," Ammen Collection (Hereinafter cited as Ammen, "Wood as Founder.").

6 "The Convention of Ninety-three," *Kappa Alpha Journal* XI (October 1893), 9.

7 Ammen, "Judge James Ward Wood," 336; idem, "Wood as Founder," 1.

8 Ibid.

9 Ibid., 2.

10 Ammen, "Judge James Ward Wood," 336.

11 Samuel Zenas Ammen, "Humphreys and Wood," Second Blank Copy Book, Ammen Collection, 46.

12 Samuel Zenas Ammen, "James Ward Wood, A Sketch," 51.

13 Ibid.

14 Dr. Olinger Crenshaw, interview by author, Lexington, Virginia, 16 April 1967.

15 Leroy Stafford Boyd to Samuel Zenas Ammen, July 15, 1918, Letter concerning Boyd's interview with James Ward Wood. Ammen Collection.

16 Leroy Stafford Boyd to Samuel Zenas Ammen, December 4, 1919. Ammen Collection.

17 Milton W. Humphreys to Samuel Zenas Ammen, June 12, 1915, testimony in Second Blank Copy Book, Ammen Collection, 46.

18 Samuel Zenas Ammen, "James Ward Wood," *Kappa Alpha Journal* XXVI (October-December 1908), 6-7. In later years the founders differed among themselves as to where on the Washington and Lee campus the fraternity was actually founded. Stanhope McClelland Scott, the last founder to survive, maintained that Kappa Alpha was organized in Wood's room in the "Cat Tail", a small building which stood to the North of Washington Hall. In the 1930s, when the fraternity wanted to erect a small plaque at the exact location of the founding, Stanhope Scott's opinion on the matter was followed, and the plaque was placed in a second floor classroom in the small building, projecting northward from Washington Hall, close to the location of the old "Cat Tail". However, during his first year at Washington College, Wood did not live at the "Cat Tail". Rather, he lived at the Tutwiler home about a mile south of Lexington, a fact confirmed by Milton W. Humphreys, who roomed with Wood at Tutwiler's, in his conversation with Dr. Ammen in 1915. Also, the Reverend William Nelson Scott, in an article that he wrote for the *Kappa Alpha Journal* of May 1898, stated that the fraternity was organized in Walsh's room in the old South Dormitory. In a letter to Dr. Ammen dated August 9, 1891, that appeared in the *Kappa Alpha Journal* of March, 1913, James Ward Wood stated: "The first meeting was held in the end room of the `South Dormitory,' then occupied by William A. Walsh, of Richmond, since disceased. Afterwards, meetings were held in the "Cat Tail". Stanhope Scott was only sixteen when he was brought into the fraternity by Wood and by his brother, William Nelson Scott. As Stanhope Scott did not enter Washington College until January of 1866, he may not have been present at the original conversation between his brother Nelson and Wood when they decided to organize the fraternity (an assumption based on the theory that the fraternity was organized in December 1865). More likely, Stanhope Scott, because of his youth at the time, did not remember, years later, the meetings in Walsh's room, but remembered instead the later meetings at the "Cat Tail". The majority of the evidence supports Walsh's room in the South Dormitory, on the site of the present Newcomb Hall, as the place of founding.

19 Dr. Stanhope McClelland Scott to G. D. Letcher, November 10, 1931, G. D. Letcher Papers, National Administrative Office, Kappa Alpha Order, Atlanta (Hereinafter cited as Letcher Papers.).

20 James Ward Wood to Samuel Zenas Ammen, August 9, 1891, printed in *Kappa Alpha Journal* XXX (March 1913), 343.

21 Dr. Stanhope McClelland Scott to G. D. Letcher, November 30, 1931. Letcher Papers.

22 William Nelson Scott to Samuel Zenas Ammen, June, 1885, quoted in *Kappa Alpha Journal* XV (May 1898), 334.

23 Milton W. Humphreys to Samuel Zenas Ammen, June 12, 1915, testimony in Second Blank Copy Book, Ammen Collection, 46.

24 Three possibilities exist as to origin of the name Kappa Alpha: Northern Kappa Alpha; "Knights of the Arch," an alleged Royal Arch Degree in Masonry; and an antebellum Southern college fraternity called Kuklos Adelphon. This question has never been resolved, in spite much speculation. Leroy S. Boyd and Samuel Zenas Ammen were especially involved in attempting to resolve the issue, but all arguments are inconclusive. Although the name may have been derived from some pre-existing organization, the fraternity had no generic connection with any previous group.

25 William Nelson Scott to Samuel Zenas Ammen, April, 1898, quoted in *Kappa Alpha Journal* XXIX (March 1913), 329.

26 Thomas Edward McCorkle, Lexington, Virginia; Robert S. Thompson, Tennessee; Robert Nelson Gillespie, Little Washington, Tennessee; Thomas Jefferson Morrison Hanson, Wytheville, Virginia; William Saville, Lexington, Virginia; and Samuel Lindsey Kirkpatrick, Alone, Virginia.

27 Ammen, "The Founding," *Kappa Alpha Journal* XV (March 1898), 333:

28 Ammen, "Dr. William Nelson Scott," *Kappa Alpha Journal* XV (May 1898), 339.

29 James Ward Wood, "Original Essay, November 26, 1886," Ammen Collection.

30 Leroy Stafford Boyd to Samuel Zenas Ammen, July 5, 1918, Letter regarding Boyd's visit with James Ward Wood, Ammen Collection.

31 Samuel Zenas Ammen, "Early History of the Alpha," *Kappa Alpha Magazine* I (April 1884), 3.

32 Samuel Zenas Ammen, "The Kappa Alpha Fraternity," *Directory of the Kappa Alpha Order, 1865-1922*, edited by W. B. Crawford (Orlando, Florida: Published by the Fraternity, 1922), 7.

33 Minutes of Alpha Chapter, Kappa Alpha Fraternity, October 17, 1866, Ammen Collection. (Hereinafter cited as Alpha Minutes.).

34 William Kavanaugh Doty, *Samuel Zenas Ammen and the Kappa Alpha Order* (Charlottesville: Suber-Arundale Company, 1922), passim.

35 Samuel Zenas Ammen, "In the Old Alpha," *Kappa Alpha Journal* XIV (January 1897), 207.

36 College Diary of Samuel Zenas Ammen, March 17, 1866. Brown Folio, Ammen Collection (Hereinafter cited as Ammen's College Diary.).

37 Ammen, "The Founding," 328.

38 Joseph S. Chick, ed., *History and Catalogue of the Kappa Alpha Fraternity* (Nashville: n. p., 1891), xx.

39 Ammen, "The Founding," 333.

40 Alpha Minutes, December 7, 1866.

41 Samuel Zenas Ammen, "History of the K. A. Fraternity and its Institutions," *Catalogue of the Kappa Alpha Fraternity, 1865-1900*, edited by Paul Murill (Charlotte: n. p., 1900), 2.

42 Ammen's College Diary, March 17, 1867.

43 Samuel Zenas Ammen with Stanhope McClelland Scott, interview quoted in *Kappa Alpha Journal* XXXVII (September 1921), 343.

44 Ammen, "Judge James Ward Wood," 337.

45 Ammen, "James Ward Wood, A Sketch."

46 Alpha Minutes, January 25, 1867.

47 Ammen, "Judge James Ward Wood," 337.

48 Ammen's College Diary, April 14, 1867.

49 Samuel Zenas Ammen, "Jo Lane Stern," *Kappa Alpha Journal* XXXVIII (November 1921), 19.

50 Samuel Zenas Ammen, "William Nelson Scott," First Blank Copy Book, Ammen Collection, 63.

51 Alpha Minutes, September 27, 1867.

52 Alpha Minutes, September 27, 1867; October 11, 1867; October 18, 1867; February 21, 1868.

53 Ibid., October 18, 1867.

54 Ibid., February 7, 1868.

55 Ibid.

56 Ibid., March 8, 1868.

57 Ibid., March 21, 1868.

58 Ibid., May 1, 1868.

59 Tazewell Taylor Hubard, "History of Beta Chapter," Blue Copy Book, KA Archives, 9.

60 Alpha Minutes, January 24, 1868.

61 Ibid.

62 Ammen's College Diary, June 16, 1868.

63 Alpha Minutes, June 16, 1868.

64 Ammen's College Diary, June 16, 1868; Ammen's Convivium Speech of 1868, Second Blank Copy Book, Ammen Collection.

65 Ammen's College Diary, July 25, 1868.

66 Alpha Minutes, November, 1868.

67 Ibid., February 8, 1869.

68 Ibid.

69 Taylor Tazewell Hubard, "History of Beta Chapter," Bound Handwritten Manuscript, KA Archives, 13.

70 Paul Murill, ed., *Catalogue of the Kappa Alpha Fraternity, 1865-1900* (Charlotte: Published by the Fraternity, 1900), 96.

71 W. B. Crawford, ed., *Directory of the Kappa Alpha Order, 1865-1922* (Orlando, Florida: Published by the Fraternity, 1922), 12.

72 Alpha Minutes, November 27, 1869.

73 Ibid., November 27, 1869; and March 24, 1870.

74 Ibid.

75 Franklin L. Riley, *General Robert E. Lee after Appotomattox* (New York: Macmillan Co., 1922), 120.

76 Jo Lane Stern to John L. Hardeman, April 27, 1870, Letter quoted in *Kappa Alpha Journal* XIX (November 1901), 174.

77 Samuel Zenas Ammen to W. B. Crawford, 1924, Ammen Collection.

78 Alpha Minutes, February 17, 1870; and April 7, 1870.

79 Samuel Zenas Ammen, "The First KA Convention," Ammen Collection.

80 Ibid.

81 Samuel Zenas Ammen, "Events and Dates of S. Z. A.'s Life," First Blank Copy Book, Ammen Collection, 66.

Chapter II
INSTITUTIONAL AND STRUCTURAL DEVELOPMENT
1870-1897

1 C. Vann Woodward, *Origins of the New South*, vol. IX of *A History of the South*, eds. E. Merton Coulter and Wendell Holmes Stephenson; (Baton Rouge: L. S. U. Press, 1951), 438.

2 Ibid., 439.

3 Burton J. Hendrick, *The Training of an American, The Earlier Life and Letters of Walter Hines Page, 1855-1913* (Boston and New York: Houghton Mifflin Co., The Riverside Press, 1928), 44-45.

4 Edwin Mims, *History of Vanderbilt University* (Nashville: Vanderbilt University Press, 1946), 78-81.

5 "A Short Sketch of KA, from 1865 to 1883," *Kappa Alpha Magazine* I (November 1883), 9-13.

6 Phillip B. Hamer, "Reminiscences," *Kappa Alpha Journal* XXI (January 1904), 321.

7 Samuel Zenas Ammen, *Kappa Alpha in '97* (Wheeling, West Virginia: Printed and Distributed under the Care of Dr. William S. Hamilton, 1897), 5.

8 John L. Hardeman, ed., *Biennial Catalogue of the Kappa Alpha Order, 1873-1875* (Macon, Georgia: Published by the Editor, 1878), 20.

9 Tazewell Taylor Hubard, "The K. C.-ship and the K. C.'s," *Kappa Alpha Journal* XI (April 1894), 332.

10 Daniel R. Neal, Jr., ed., *Catalogue of the Kappa Alpha Order, 1865-1878* (Parkersburg, West Virginia: Published by the Editor, 1878), 8.

11 Ibid.

12 Ibid., passim.

13 Hubard, "The K. C. -ship and the K. C.'s," 332.

14 *Minutes of the Ninth Convention of the Kappa Alpha Order, held with Kappa Chapter, Mercer University, Macon, Georgia,* 1878, KA Archives, 6.

15 "Beta Letter Book I," KA Archives, passim.

16 William Sprigg Hamilton, "Brief Biographies of the Editors of the Kappa Alpha Order," Bound Typed Manuscript, KA Archives, 1.

17 "Editorial Notes," *Kappa Alpha Journal* I (February 1879), 37.

18 *Minutes of the KA Fraternity, held at Richmond, Virginia, June 12-14, 1883*, KA Archives, passim. *Minutes of the 13th Biennial Convention, Nashville, Tennessee, October 1, 1885,* KA Archives, 7.

19 Ibid.

20 Phillip B. Hammer, "Editorial," *Kappa Alpha Magazine* I (November 1883), 5.

21 *Kappa Alpha Magazine* I, passim.

22 "The KA State Association of South Carolina," *Kappa Alpha Magazine* I (November 1884), 35-36.

23 *Kappa Alpha Magazine*, vols. I and II, passim.

24 *Minutes of the 13th Biennial Convention, Nashville, Tennessee, October 1, 1885,* KA Archives, 4-5.

25 Samuel Zenas Ammen, "The Kappa Alpha Fraternity," *Directory of the Kappa Alpha Order, 1865-1922,* ed. W. B. Crawford, 28-29.

26 *Minutes of the 13th Biennial Convention,* Nashville, Tennessee, October 1, 1885, KA Archives, 9.

27 "Masthead," *Kappa Alpha Journal* III (October 1886), 2.

28 Murill, *Catalogue of the Kappa Alpha Fraternity, 1865-1900,* 18.

29 Ibid., 14.

30 *Minutes of the 15th KA Convention, held at Augusta, Georgia, September 11th, 12th, and 13th, 1889,* KA Archives, 10, 11, and 14.

31 Ammen, "Events and Dates of S. Z. A.'s Life," 66.

32 Ibid., 67.

33 Murill, *Catalogue of the Kappa Alpha Fraternity, 1865-1900*, 21.

34 William Sprigg Hamilton, "Brief Biographies of the Grand Historians of the Kappa Alpha Order," Bound Typed Manuscript, KA Archives, 20-22.

35 Samuel Zenas Ammen, ed., *Minutes of the Eighteenth Biennial Convention of the Kappa Alpha Order, held at the Atlanta, Georgia, September 25th, 26th, 27th, 1895* (Baltimore: The Sun Book and Job Printing Office, 1895), 10.

36 Samuel Zenas Ammen, "Convention at Washington vs. Jones' Baseless Charges, Condemned Verner Jones as a Liar," unpublished handwritten manuscript, Ammen collection. This intrafraternal political squabble, referred to in fraternity records as the "Jones Rebellion" of 1897, involved personalities more than it did issues. Previous to Ammen's election as K. C. the small group of alumni at Nashville through their control of the *Journal* and several fraternity offices, had enjoyed wide influence within the fraternity. Increasingly frustrated by Ammen's rather high handed methods, they attempted in 1897 to dethrone Ammen's hand picked successor, Dr. William S. Hamilton. The instigator of the controversy was Keeble's successor as editor, Verner M. Jones. Intense mudslinging ensued, with both sides eventually resorting to diatribes and pamphleteering. Hamilton, at Ammen's instigation, removed Jones as editor and then resigned as Knight Commander. The special Washington convention of 1898 resolved the matter by electing a new K. C. and a new editor, both of whom were relatively unallied to either side. The convention also dismissed Jones' charges against Hamilton and vindicated Ammen by giving him a vote of appreciation. Nonetheless, the Jones and Ammen factions continued to squabble for many years.

37 "Editorial," *Kappa Alpha Journal* VII (January 1890), 191.

38 John Bell Keeble, "Rushing," *Kappa Alpha Journal* IX (December 1891), 167.

39 "Editorial," *Kappa Alpha Journal* X (December 1892), 162-164.

40 "The Chapter House System," *Kappa Alpha Journal* XIII (December 1895), 143-146.

41 Samuel Zenas Ammen to William Sprigg Hamilton, July 21, 1895, Hamilton Letter Box I, KA Archives.

Chapter III
THE ROMANTIC MIND OF THE KA

1 Samuel Zenas Ammen, "R. E. Lee and Etc.," Second Blank Copy Book, Unpublished Manuscript, Ammen Collection, 91.

2 Samuel Zenas Ammen to Tazewell Taylor Hubard, March 6, 1895, Hubard's Manuscript Letter Books, No. 5, 115, KA Archives.

3 Samuel Zenas Ammen to William Kavanaugh Doty, July 21, 1922, quoted in Doty, *Samuel Zenas Ammen and the Kappa Alpha Order*, 59.

4 Samuel Zenas Ammen, "Study the Classics," *Kappa Alpha Journal* I (December 1879), 81-86.

5 Ammen, "The Kappa Alpha Fraternity," *Directory of the Kappa Alpha Order, 1865-1922*, ed. W. B. Crawford, 13-14.

6 Doty, *Samuel Zenas Ammen*, passim.

7 Ammen, "Events and Dates of S .Z. A.'s Life," 66-68.

8 Samuel Zenas Ammen, "Robert E. Lee and Etc.," 91-93.

9 Doty, *Samuel Zenas Ammen*, 9-10, 15-18, and 21.

10 Samuel Zenas Ammen, "Extracts from Ammen's College Diary, 1866-1868," Brown Folio, Ammen Collection.

11 Doty, *Samuel Zenas Ammen*, passim.

12 Samuel Zenas Ammen, "Early History of the Alpha," *Kappa Alpha Magazine* I (April 1884), 1-2.

13 Doty, *Samuel Zenas Ammen*, 16.

14 Ammen, "Early History of the Alpha," 1-2.

15 Ammen, "Speech at Convivium, June 18, 1868."

16 Samuel Zenas Ammen, "The Kappa Alpha Lover," *Kappa Alpha Journal* IX (June 1892), 385-386.

17 "Alpha Chapter Minutes," October 17, 1866, Ammen Collection.

18 Samuel Zenas Ammen, *Green Book of 1870*, Ammen Collection; _____, *Constitution and Ritual of 1893*, KA Archives. Because of the secret nature of these documents, the writer cannot indulge in direct quotation or exact citation. Thus, the reader will have to take the writer's word for it that the ideas described are the ideas contained therein.

19 Samuel Zenas Ammen, *Constitution and Ritual of 1893*.

20 Samuel Zenas Ammen, "Innocence, An Essay Delivered to Alpha Chapter, December 25, 1866," Second Blank Copy Book, Ammen Collection, 75-82.

21 Samuel Zenas Ammen, "A Speech Made by S. Z. A. when Entering His Term as I of Alpha Chapter," First Blank Copy Book, Ammen Collection, 51-55.

22 John Bell Keeble, "Editorial," *Kappa Alpha Journal* VIII (February 1890), 233-235.

23 Samuel Zenas Ammen, *Brown Book of 1874*, edited by John L. Hardeman, Ammen Collection, 7. This is the 1874 edition of the ritual and constitution, both of which in the early editions were bound together.

24 Walter Weidman Brown, "Preliminary Degree," *Minutes of the Kappa Alpha Fraternity, held at Richmond, Virginia, June 12-14, 1883*, KA Archives, 13.

25 Verner M. Jones, "Current Topics," *Kappa Alpha Journal* XII (March 1895), 253.

26 John Bell Keeble, "Choose Carefully," *Kappa Alpha Journal* VIII (October 1890), 11-15.

27 John Bell Keeble, "The Coming Fraternity," *Kappa Alpha Journal*, XII (June 1895), 327.

28 Ammen, "College Diary," February 27, 1868.

29 Samuel Zenas Ammen, "A Kappa Alpha; What is Expected of a K. A.," undelivered speech, March 30, 1906, KA Archives.

Chapter IV
THE PHANTOM OF NORTHERN EXTENSION

1 "To the Tune of `Mr. Dooley'," *Kappa Alpha Journal* III (February 1905), 333.

2 Ammen "The Kappa Alpha Fraternity," *Directory of the Kappa Alpha Order, 1865-1900*, 1.

3 Ibid., 3.

4 Ibid., 36.

5 Ammen, *Kappa Alpha in '97*, 5.

6 "Union with Northern Kappa Alpha, the Other Side," *Kappa Alpha Magazine* II (November 1884), 6-7.

7 Danial R. Neal to James Leighton Hubard, July 14, 1885, Beta Letter Book I, KA Archives, 70-71.

8 Ibid.

9 Leroy S. Boyd to Samuel Zenas Ammen, July 15, 1918, Ammen Collection; William Nelson Scott to Samuel Zenas Ammen, June 23, 1885, cited in *Kappa Alpha Journal* XXIX (March 1913), 346. Both William Nelson Scott and James Ward Wood testified many years later that they had not heard of Northern KA until after they had fully conceived their organization.

10 Samuel Zenas Ammen, "The First KA Convention," unpublished manuscript, Ammen Collection.

11 "A Short Sketch of the Kappa Alpha Fraternity from 1865 to 1883," *Kappa Alpha Magazine* I (November 1883), 11.

12 Hardeman, ed., *Biennial Catalogue of Kappa Alpha Order, 1873-1875*, 17.

13 *Minutes of the Ninth Annual Convention of the Kappa Alpha Order, held with Kappa Alpha Chapter, Mercer University, Macon, Georgia, July 5, 1878*, KA Archives, 5.

14 *Minutes of the Kappa Alpha Fraternity, held at Richmond, Virginia, June 12-14, 1883*, KA Archives, 7.

15 James W. Morris, "Union with Northern Kappa Alpha," *Kappa Alpha Magazine* I (January 1884), 1-4.

16 Ibid., 4.

17 Warren Akin Candler, "Has Our Order an Aim?," *Kappa Alpha Magazine* II (November 1884), 1-2.

18 R. L. M. Parks, "Union with Northern Kappa Alpha," *Kappa Alpha Magazine* I (April 1884), 11.

19 Ammen, "The Early History of the Alpha," 6.

20 "A Few Voluntary Remarks," *Kappa Alpha Magazine* I (April 1884), "Union with Northern Kappa Alpha, the Other Side," *Kappa Alpha Magazine* II (November 1884), 6-7.

21 Francis W. Shepardson, ed., *Baird's Manual of American College Fraternities* (Menasha, Wisconsin: The Collegiate Press, George Banta Publishing Company, 1935), 66, 122, 171-172, 182, and 198.

22 Neal, *Catalogue of the Kappa Alpha Order*, 1865-1878, 25.

23 William Sprigg Hamilton, "Kappa Alpha and Northern Extension," Unpublished Typed Manuscript, n.d., Hamilton Collection.

24 H. H. White, "Editorial," *Kappa Alpha Journal* III (March 1886), 17.

25 Murill, *Catalogue of the Kappa Alpha Fraternity, 1865-1900*, 21.

26 Samuel Zenas Ammen, ed., *Minutes of the Seventeenth Biennial Convention of the Kappa Alpha Order, Held in Richmond, Virginia September 13th, 14th, and 15th, 1893* (Baltimore: The Sun Book and Job Printing Office, 1893), 7.

27 Samuel Zenas Ammen to Tazewell Taylor Hubard, March 6, 1895, Hubard's Letter Book V, KA Archives.

28 Samuel Zenas Ammen, ed., *Minutes of the 18th Biennial Convention, Kappa Alpha Order, Atlanta, Georgia*, September 25, 1895 (Baltimore: The Sun Office, 1895), 9 (Hereinafter cited as *Minutes of 1895.*).

29 Samuel Zenas Ammen, "The Phantom of Northern Extension," *Kappa Alpha Journal* III (February 1886), 15. Samuel Zenas Ammen, "Northern Extension,"*Kappa Alpha Journal* XI (February 1894), 238-241. Samuel Zenas Ammen, "Northern Extension, Some Questions," *Kappa Alpha Journal* XXI (January 1895), 114-119.

30 Samuel Zenas Ammen, "Knight Commander's Report," *Minutes of 1895*, 25-27.

31 Ammen to Hubard, March 6, 1895.

32 H. H. White to Samuel Zenas Ammen, October 12, 1891, Samuel Zenas Ammen, Knight Commander's Diary, 1891-1895, Ammen Collection.

33 John Bell Keeble, "Editorial," *Kappa Alpha Journal* VII (April 1890), 351-353.

34 John Bell Keeble, "Northern Extension," *Kappa Alpha Journal* XIII (October 1895), 84-85.

35 Samuel Zenas Ammen to Tazewell Taylor Hubard, October 1, 1895, Hubard's Letter Book V, KA Archives.

36 John Bell Keeble, "Valedictory," *Kappa Alpha Journal* XIII (March 1896), 250-251.

37 Samuel Zenas Ammen, Second Blank Copy Book, Ammen Collection, 91-93.

38 Samuel Zenas Ammen to D. R. Neal, October 13, 1891, Hubard's Letter Book III, KA Archives.

39 Samuel M. Wilson,"Editorial," *Kappa Alpha Journal* XV (March 1898), 288-289.

Chapter V
THE LOST CAUSE, SOUTHERN HISTORY, AND ROBERT E. LEE

1 Samuel Zenas Ammen, "History of the Kappa Alpha Order, its Origin and Development," *History and Catalogue of the Kappa Alpha Fraternity*, ed. Joseph S. Chick (Nashville: Published by the Fraternity, 1891), xxiv.

2 "The Present South," *Kappa Alpha Journal* IV (March 1887), 5.

3 "Public Schools in the South," *Kappa Alpha Journal* I (August 1879), 56.

4 "Jefferson Davis at Montgomery, 1861-1886," *Kappa Alpha Journal* IV (October 1886), 6.

5 Greenlee D. Letcher, "The Jefferson Davis Memorial," *Kappa Alpha Journal* VII (May 1890), 374, quoting the Lexington, Virginia *Gazette*, January 9, 1890.

6 William Sprigg Hamilton, "I Will Live and Not Die," *Kappa Alpha Journal* VII (October 1889), 3.

7 Ibid.

8 "The Spirit of Chivalry," *Kappa Alpha Journal* XV (March 1898), 217.

9 Ibid.

10 Ibid.

11 "Jefferson Davis at Montgomery," *Kappa Alpha Journal* IV (October 1886), 8-9.

12 "The Present South," *Kappa Alpha Journal* IV (March 1887), 6.

13 W. M. Dupuy, "Address of Welcome to the 13th Biennial Kappa Alpha Convention," *Kappa Alpha Journal* III (November 1885), 8.

14 Horace Henry White, "The South," *Kappa Alpha Journal* IV (February 1887), 11-12.

15 Samuel Zenas Ammen, "The Kappa Alpha Fraternity," *Directory of the Kappa Alpha Order, 1865-1922*, 13-14.

16 "The Present South," *Kappa Alpha Journal* IV (March 1887), 6.

17 "Our Origin," *Kappa Alpha Journal* IV (April 1887), 7.

18 Ammen, *Kappa Alpha in '97*, 11.

19 R. E. Pritchard, "Our Point of View — R. E. Lee," *Kappa Alpha Journal* XVIII (January 1901), 266.

20 Pratt A. Brown, "R. E. Lee — A Toast," *Kappa Alpha Journal* XVIII (May 1901), 483-485. "The Twenty-first Convention," *Kappa Alpha Journal*, XIX (September 1901), 6.

21 Rion McKissick, "The Semi-centennial Convention, *Kappa Alpha Journal* XXXIII (March 1916), 119-146.

22 Thomas Dixon, Jr., *The Man In Grey* (New York: Grosset and Dunlap, 1921), ii.

23 John Temple Graves, "Robert E. Lee," *Kappa Alpha Journal* XI (January 1924), 146-147.

24 Samuel Zenas Ammen to W. B. Crawford, September 23, 1924, Ammen Collection.

25 Frank H. Myers, "Washington and the Convention," *Kappa Alpha Journal* XI (January 1924), 127.

BIBLIOGRAPHY

Samuel Zenas Ammen wrote the ritual and early laws of the Kappa Alpha Fraternity, largely evolved the structure of its organization in the first half-century of its existence, took the main part in expanding and revising the ritual over a long period of years, and served as Knight Commander from 1869 to 1871 and again from 1891 to 1897. He also served as the unofficial historian of the fraternity from the very beginning until his death in 1929. Ammen wrote practically all articles in the early volumes of the *Kappa Alpha Journal* and in the fraternity catalogues dealing with fraternity history. And, except for a few letters and an occasional article written by the Scott brothers, Wood, and Stern, and the Minutes of Alpha Chapter, Ammen's writings and recollections constitute the main body of primary sources dealing with the founding and very early history of the fraternity. Consequently, much of the original source material is colored by Ammen's opinions, biases, interpretations, and conclusions. In later life, Ammen sought to vindicate his position as chief designer of the organization, and therefore, many of the sources from that period contain elaborations of his role as founder as well as justifications for his actions, his Southern bias, and his heavy influence on the evolution of the ritual. Thus, for many years, Ammen further influenced the organization by being the sole interpreter of its history.

I. PRIMARY SOURCES

A. MANUSCRIPTS

Samuel Zenas Ammen Collection, 1866-1926. Contemporary sources and subsequent manuscript writings concerning the early history of the Kappa Alpha Fraternity, as well as occasional writings dealing with fraternity affairs through the mid 1920s. National Administrative Office, Kappa Alpha Order, Lexington, Virginia.

William Sprigg Hamilton Collection. Manuscript material relevant to the later history of the Kappa Alpha Order, with a few items relevant to early Kappa Alpha history. The major body of material was written between 1936 and 1954, during the time Hamilton was Archivist of the fraternity, National Administrative Office, Kappa Alpha Order, Lexington, Virginia.

Kappa Alpha Archives, 1870-1994. Several hundred volumes containing various fraternity records and virtually all fraternity publications from the very beginning to the present date. National Administrative Office, Kappa Alpha Order, Lexington, Virginia.

Greenlee Davidson Letcher Papers, early 1890s through mid 1930s. Containing correspondence of the 1920s and 1930s in regard to the founding date controversy. National Administrative Office, Kappa Alpha Order, Lexington, Virginia.

B. PERIODICALS

Kappa Alpha Journal, 1869-1940, 56 Volumes. The official fraternity magazine. From 1883 to 1885, known as the *Kappa Alpha Magazine*. Published in various Southern cities during its history. Originally established as a literary magazine in 1879, failed in late 1879, publication resumed in 1883, as an organ devoted to fraternity news and issues. National Administrative Office, Kappa Alpha Order, Lexington, Virginia.

C. PERIODICAL ARTICLES

"A Few Voluntary Remarks," *Kappa Alpha Magazine* I (April 1884), 9.

"Against Family Qualifications," *Kappa Alpha Journal* IV (October 1886), 21-22.

Ammen, Samuel Zenas, "Dr. William Nelson Scott," *Kappa Alpha Journal* XV (May 1898), 339-341.

———, "Dr. William Nelson Scott," *Kappa Alpha Journal* XXXVII (November 1920), 2-5.

———, "Early History of the Alpha," *Kappa Alpha Magazine* I (April 1884), 1-7.

———, "In the Old Alpha," *Kappa Alpha Journal* XIV (January 1897), 206-211.

———, "James Ward Wood," *Kappa Alpha Journal* XVII (October-December 1908), 6-7.

———, "James Ward Wood," *Kappa Alpha Journal* XXXVII (May 1921), 218-221.

———, "Jo Lane Stern," *Kappa Alpha Journal* XXXVIII (November 1921), 19-22.

———, "Judge James Ward Wood," *Kappa Alpha Journal* XV (May 1898), 335-339.

———, "Northern Extension," *Kappa Alpha Journal* XI (February 1894), 238-241.

———, "Northern Extension, Some Questions," *Kappa Alpha Journal* XII (January 1895), 114-119.

———, "Stanhope McClelland Scott and W. A. Walsh," *Kappa Alpha Journal* XV (May 1898), 341-342.

———, "Study the Classics," *Kappa Alpha Journal* I (December 1879), 81-86.

———, "The Founding," *Kappa Alpha Journal* XV (May 1898), 226-235.

———, "The Founders of Kappa Alpha, Walsh and S. M. Scott," *Kappa Alpha Journal* XXXVII (September 1921), 340-344.

———, "The Kappa Alpha Lover," *Kappa Alpha Journal* IX (June 1892), 385-388.

———, "The Phantom of Northern Extension," *Kappa Alpha Journal* III (February 1886), 15.

"An Open Letter, The Family Qualifications," *Kappa Alpha Journal* III (November 1885), 9-10.

"A Short Sketch of the Kappa Alpha Fraternity from 1865 to 1883," *Kappa Alpha Magazine* I (November 1883), 11.

Brown, Pratt A., "R. E. Lee — A Toast," *Kappa Alpha Journal* XVIII (May 1901), 483-485.

Candler, Warren Akin, "Has Our Order an Aim?" *Kappa Alpha Magazine* II (November 1884), 12.

"Convention of 1893," *Kappa Alpha Journal* XI (October 1893), 9.

Dupuy, W. M., "Address of Welcome to the 13th Biennial KA Convention," *Kappa Alpha Journal* III (November 1885), 8.

"Editorial Notes," *Kappa Alpha Journal* I (February 1879), 57.

Graves, John Temple, "Robert Edward Lee," *Kappa Alpha Journal* XI (January 1924), 146-147.

Hamer, Phillip B., "Editorial," *Kappa Alpha Magazine* I (November 1883), 5.

_____, "Reminiscences," *Kappa Alpha Journal* XXI (January 1904), 321.

Hamilton, William Sprigg, "Will Live and Not Die," *Kappa Alpha Journal* VII (October 1889), 3.

Hobson, G. A., "The Harp of Life," *Kappa Alpha Journal* III (October 1885), 3-8.

Hubard, Tazewell Taylor, "The K. C.-ship and the K. C.'s," *Kappa Alpha Journal* XI (April 1894), 321-342.

"Jefferson Davis at Montgomery, 1861-1886," *Kappa Alpha Journal* IV (October 1886), 6-9.

Jones, Verner M., "Current Topics," *Kappa Alpha Journal* XII (March 1895), 253.

Keeble, John Bell, "Choose Carefully," *Kappa Alpha Journal* VIII (October 1890), 11-15.

_____, "Editorial," *Kappa Alpha Journal* VII (January 1890), 191.

_____, "Editorial," *Kappa Alpha Journal* VIII (February 1890), 233-235.

_____, "Editorial," *Kappa Alpha Journal* X (December, 1892), 162-164.

_____, "Rushing," *Kappa Alpha Journal* IX (December 1891), 167-168.

_____, "The Coming Fraternity," *Kappa Alpha Journal* XII (June 1895), 327.

_____, "The Ideal Fraternity," *Kappa Alpha Journal* IX (February 1892), 220-223.

Kilgo, Pierce F., "The Mind of Man," *Kappa Alpha Journal* V (November 1887), 3-8.

Letcher, Greenlee D., "The Jefferson Davis Memorial," *Kappa Alpha Journal* VII (May 1890), 374. Quoting the Lexington, Virginia *Gazette* of 9 January 1890.

McKissick, Rion, "The Semi-centennial Convention," *Kappa Alpha Journal* XXXIII (March 1916), 119-146.

Morris, James W., "Union with Northern Kappa Alpha," *Kappa Alpha Magazine* I (January 1884), 1-4.

Myers, Frank H., "Washington and the Convention," *Kappa Alpha Journal* XL (January 1924), 127.

"Our Origins," *Kappa Alpha Journal* IV (April 1887), 7.

Parks, R. L, M., "Union with Northern Kappa Alpha," *Kappa Alpha Magazine* I (April 1884), 11.

Pritchard, R. E., "Our Point of View — R. E. Lee," *Kappa Alpha Journal* XVIII (January 1901), 266.

"Public Schools in the South," *Kappa Alpha Journal* I (August 1879), 56.

Scott, William Nelson, "Early Reminiscences of 'Old Alpha' Chapter, K. A.," *Kappa Alpha Journal* XV (May 1898), 342-344.

"Some Early KA History," *Kappa Alpha Journal* XXIX (March 1913), 343-347.

Stern, Jo Lane, "Letter from Jo Lane Stern to John L. Hardeman, April 27, 1870," *Kappa Alpha Journal* XIX (November 1901), 174.

"The Chapter House System," *Kappa Alpha Journal* XIII (December 1895), 143-146.

"The K. A. State Association of South Carolina," *Kappa Alpha Magazine* I (November 1884), 35-36.

"The Present South," *Kappa Alpha Magazine* IV (March 1887), 5-8.

"The Spirit of Chivalry," *Kappa Alpha Journal* XV (March 1895), 213-218.

"The Twenty-first Convention," *Kappa Alpha Journal* XIX (September 1901), 6.

"To the Tune of Mr. Dooley," *Kappa Alpha Journal* XXII (February 1905), 333.

"Union with Northern Kappa Alpha, the Other Side," *Kappa Alpha Magazine* II (November 1884), 6-7.

White, Horace Henry, "Editorial," *Kappa Alpha Journal* III (March 1886), 17.

_____, "The South," *Kappa Alpha Journal* IV (February 1887), 11-12.

Willoughby, Julius E., "The Ideal to be Attained," *Kappa Alpha Journal* XVIII (December 1895), 115-117.

D. PAMPHLETS

Ammen, Samuel Zenas, *Kappa Alpha in '97*. Wheeling, West Virginia: Printed and Distributed under the Care of Dr. William S. Hamilton, 1897.

Hardeman, John L. *General Catalogue, K. A. O., From 1865 to 1873.* n. p., 1873.

_____, *Biennial Catalogue of Kappa Alpha Order, 1873-1875.* n. p., 1875.

Neal, Daniel R., *General Catalogue, From 1865 to 1878, Kappa Alpha Order*. Parkersburg, West Virginia: George Elletson Printer, Court Square, 1878.

E. BOOKS CONTAINING PRIMARY SOURCE MATERIAL

Chick, Joseph S. ed., *History and Catalogue of the Kappa Alpha Fraternity*. Nashville: Published by the Fraternity, 1891.

Crawford, W. B. ed., *Directory of the Kappa Alpha Order, 1865-1922*. Orlando, Florida: Published by the Fraternity, 1922.

Doty, William Kavanaugh, *Samuel Zenas Ammen and the Kappa Alpha Order*. Charlottesville: Suber-Arundale Company, 1922.
Murill, Paul ed., *Catalogue of the Kappa Alpha Fraternity, 1865-1900*. Charlotte: Published by the Fraternity, 1900.
Riley, Franklin L. ed., *General Lee After Appomattox*. New York: The Macmillan Company, 1922.

F. PRIVATE AND ESOTERIC SOURCES
NOT AVAILABLE TO THE PUBLIC

Ammen, Samuel Zenas, *Green Book of 1870*. Milburn, Kentucky: Published by the author, 1870.
_____, *Ritual and Constitution of 1874*. Edited by John L. Hardeman. n. p., 1874.
_____, *Ritual and Constitution, 1893*. n. p., 1893.

G. INTERVIEWS

Crenshaw, Dr. Olinger, Chairman of the Department of History, Washington and Lee University, interview by author, 16 April 1967, Lexington, Virginia, privately held.
Feller, Richard T., Senior Councilor, Kappa Alpha Order, interview by author, 26 October 1967, Washington, D.C., privately held.
Foresman, Henry J., Knight Commander, Kappa Alpha Order, interview by author, 16 April 1967, Lexington, Virginia, privately held.
Forester, William E., Executive Secretary, Kappa Alpha Order, interview by author, 20-24 March 1967, Atlanta, Georgia, privately held.

II. SECONDARY WORKS

A. BOOKS

Baird, W. Raymond, *American College Fraternities*. Philadelphia: J. B. Lippincott and Company, 1879.
Boley, Henry, *Lexington in Old Virginia*. Richmond: Garrett and Massie, 1936.
Cash, Wilbur J., *The Mind of the South*. New York: Vintage Books, 1941.
Coulter, E. Merton, *College Life in the Old South*. New York: n. p., 1928.
Coulter, E. Merton and Wendell Holmes Stephenson, eds., *A History of the South*, Volume IX. *Origins of the New South* by Comer Vann Woodward. Baton Rouge: Louisiana State University Press, 1951.
Couoer, William, *One Hundred Years at VMI*. Richmond: Garrett and Massie, 1939.
Dixon, Thomas, *The Man in Grey*. New York: Grosset and Dunlap, 1921.
Duncan, James L., ed., *Kappa Alpha Pledge Manual*. Atlanta: National Administrative Office, Kappa Alpha Order, 1965.
Eaton, Clement, *The Mind of the Old South*. Baton Rouge: Louisiana State University Press, 1967.

Freeman, Douglas Southall, *R. E. Lee*, Volume IV. New York: Charles Scribner's Sons, 1935.
Gaines, Francis Pendleton, *Lee, The Final Achievement, 1865-1870*. New York: New York Southern Society, 1933.
_____, *The Southern Plantation*. New York: Columbia University Press, 1925.
Gildersleeve, Basil L., *Creed of the Old South*. New York: n. p., 1910.
Hendrick, Burton J., *The Training of an American, The Earlier Life and Letters of Walter Hines Page, 1855-1913*. Boston and New York: Houghton Mifflin Co., The Riverside Press, 1928.
Lasher, George Starr, ed., *Baird's Manual of American College Fraternities*. Menasha, Wisconsin: The Collegiate Press, 1957.
Mims, Edwin, *History of Vanderbilt University*. Nashville: Vanderbilt University Press, 1946.
Murray, Henry Alexander, ed., *Myth and Mythmaking*. New York: G. Braziller, 1960.
Osterweis, Rollin G., *Romanticism and Nationalism in the Old South*. n. p., n. d.
Sebeok, Thomas A., *Myth A Symposium*. Bloomington: Indiana University Press, 1955.
Sheldon, Henry D., *Student Life and Customs*. New York: D. Appleton and Company, 1901.
Shepardson, Francis W., ed., *Baird's Manual of American College Fraternities*. Menasha, Wisconsin: The Collegiate Press, George Banta Publishing Company, 1935.

B. ARTICLES

Boyd, Leroy Stafford, "The Founding of Kappa Alpha," *Kappa Alpha Journal* XLIII (March 1927), 206-210.
Gist, Noel P., "Secret Societies, A Cultural Study of Fraternalism in the United States," *University of Missouri Studies* XV (October 1940).
Locke, Howard P., "The Story of Kappa Alpha." In *Kappa Alpha Pledge Manual*. ed. James L. Duncan, Atlanta: National Administrative Office, Kappa Alpha Order, 1965.
Tindall, George Brown, "Southern Mythology." In *The Idea of the South*, ed. Frank Everson Vandiver, Chicago: Published for William Marsh Rice University by the University of Chicago Press, 1964.

www.ingramcontent.com/pod-product-compliance
Lightning Source LLC
Chambersburg PA
CBHW070454090426
42735CB00012B/2549